Were 364 Economists All Wrong?

Were 364 Economists All Wrong?

EDITED BY PHILIP BOOTH

iea

The Institute of Economic Affairs

First published in Great Britain in 2006 by
The Institute of Economic Affairs
2 Lord North Street
Westminster
London SW1P 3LB
in association with Profile Books Ltd

The mission of the Institute of Economic Affairs is to improve public understanding of the fundamental institutions of a free society, with particular reference to the role of markets in solving economic and social problems.

A CIP catalogue record for this book is available from the British Library.

ISBN 0 255 36588 6

Many IEA publications are translated into languages other than English or are reprinted. Permission to translate or to reprint should be sought from the Director General at the address above.

Typeset in Stone by MacGuru Ltd
info@macguru.org.uk
Printed and bound in Great Britain by Hobbs the Printers

CONTENTS

THE AUTHORS

Philip Booth

Philip Booth is Editorial and Programme Director at the Institute of Economic Affairs and Professor of Insurance and Risk Management at the Sir John Cass Business School, City University. Before joining the IEA he was Associate Dean of Cass Business School and was a special adviser to the Bank of England on financial stability issues. He has published books and journal articles in the fields of social insurance, regulation, investment and finance, and actuarial science. He is joint editor (with Kent Matthews) of *Issues in Monetary Policy: The relationship between money and financial markets*, published by Wiley in association with the IEA. Philip Booth is editor of *Economic Affairs*, published by the IEA, and Associate Editor of the *British Actuarial Journal*.

Tim Congdon

Professor Tim Congdon was a member of the Treasury Panel of Independent Forecasters (the so-called 'six wise men'), which advised the Chancellor of the Exchequer on economic policy between 1992 and 1997. He founded Lombard Street Research in 1989 and was its Chief Economist until 2005. He has been a visiting professor at the Cardiff Business School and the Sir John

Cass Business School, City University. He has written a number of books on monetary policy and contributes widely to the financial press. He was awarded the CBE for services to economic debate in 1997. Tim Congdon is a member of the IEA Shadow Monetary Policy Committee.

David Laws

David Laws was born in 1965, and studied economics at King's College, Cambridge, between 1984 and 1987. He graduated from Cambridge with double first-class honours. David worked in the City of London for JP Morgan and Co. between 1987 and 1992, and for Barclays de Zoete Wedd between 1992 and 1994. He was Economics Adviser and Director of Policy and Research for the Liberal Democrats, 1994–99. David was elected MP for Yeovil constituency in 2001; he served on the Treasury Select Committee from 2001 to 2003, and was Liberal Democrat Shadow Chief Secretary from 2003 to 2005. Since 2005 he has been the Liberal Democrat Work and Pensions spokesman.

Patrick Minford

Patrick Minford has been Professor of Economics at Cardiff Business School, Cardiff University, since October 1997. He was a member of the Monopolies and Mergers Commission (1990–96), one of HM Treasury's Panel of Independent Forecasters (the 'six wise men') between January 1993 and December 1996, and received a CBE for services to economics in 1996. He is author of numerous books and articles on exchange rates, unemployment, housing and macroeconomics. He founded and directs the Liverpool Research

Group in Macroeconomics, which has published forecasts based on the Liverpool Model of the UK since 1979. Patrick Minford is a member of the IEA Shadow Monetary Policy Committee.

Stephen Nickell

Stephen Nickell has served on the Monetary Policy Committee of the Bank of England since 1 June 2000. He has recently completed a term as president of the Royal Economic Society. He is also a fellow of the British Academy and of the Econometric Society, as well as being a member of the International Board of Advisers of the Tinbergen Institute (Amsterdam) and a member of the Council of the European Economic Association. Previously, he was School Professor of Economics at the LSE (retired September 2005) and before that Professor of Economics and director of the Institute of Economics and Statistics, University of Oxford, and a Professorial Fellow of Nuffield College. He has acted as academic consultant for various government bodies including HM Treasury, the Manpower Services Commission and the DHSS. Professor Nickell gained a BSc in mathematics from Pembroke College, Cambridge, in 1965. He also gained an MSc in mathematical economics and econometrics at the LSE in 1970.

Maurice Peston

Maurice Peston is emeritus professor at Queen Mary College, University of London. He was educated at LSE and Princeton. He has written several books and academic papers. He has been economic adviser at the Ministry of Defence, HM Treasury, the Department of Education, and the Department of Prices. He has served on numerous public bodies, frequently as chairman, and has also been chairman of the pools panel. He has been a peer since 1987.

Derek Scott

Derek Scott was special adviser to Denis Healey at HM Treasury from 1976 to 1979 and economic adviser to Tony Blair at 10 Downing Street from May 1997 to December 2003. Between these two periods in government he worked in the private sector as chief economist at Shell UK, International Policy Adviser at Shell International and, between 1984 and 1997, Director of European Economics at Barclays de Zoete Wedd.

Geoffrey Wood

Geoffrey Wood is Professor of Economics at the Sir John Cass Business School, City University. He is a graduate of Aberdeen and Essex universities, and has worked in the Federal Reserve System, the Bank of England and at several universities in Britain and overseas. He has authored, co-authored or edited over twenty books and has published over one hundred academic papers. His fields of interest are monetary economics, monetary history and financial regulation.

FOREWORD

IEA Readings 60 is published on the 25th anniversary of the letter from 364 economists to *The Times*. The letter protested against the government's fiscal and monetary policy in general and against the 1981 Budget in particular.

There is a story (maybe apocryphal) that, not long after *The Times* published its letter from the 364 economists, Margaret Thatcher was asked in debate whether she could name two economists who agreed with her. Margaret Thatcher replied that she could, and named Alan Walters and Patrick Minford. On returning to Downing Street, a civil servant said to her, 'It is a good job he did not ask you to name three.' This anecdote illustrates how much opposition there was in 1981 to fiscal and monetary policies that would today be regarded as mainstream. Indeed, the policies that were followed in the early 1980s were not just necessary to achieve their stated objectives of lower inflation, fiscal prudence and lower interest rates, they were arguably essential to prevent the economic chaos that arises from unmanageable levels of government borrowing and debt. It is easy to forget just how precarious Britain's financial situation was in the late 1970s. Both the national debt and the price level had doubled in a five-year period up to 1979. These problems were pressing priorities. If actions such as the 1981 Budget had not been taken, and if they had not been followed through to their conclusion, it is difficult to imagine what the consequences would have been.

A relatively small number of economists, including two authors of chapters in this monograph, Professor Tim Congdon and Professor Patrick Minford, as well as Professor Sir Alan Walters, an IEA Honorary Fellow, were vocal in support of the policies underlying the 1981 Budget and were close to the heart of their development. The open letter from the 364 economists was, indirectly, an attack on their academic stature – particularly given the statement that there was 'no basis in economic theory or supporting evidence' for the policy that the Budget was seeking to implement. If, today, one rejects the message of the 364 economists, even with the benefit of hindsight, one must particularly admire their opponents for swimming against the intellectual tide and making the case for theories that were deeply unfashionable in the UK. Similarly, one can only admire the convictions of a few politicians of the period who could have pursued an alternative course and avoided the intense criticism from intellectual elites that has remained with them throughout their lives.

In this monograph, we have brought together a number of economists to discuss the theoretical and political aspects of the 1981 Budget. Three of the authors (Professor Tim Congdon, Professor Patrick Minford and Professor Geoffrey Wood) made strong public statements against the 364 in 1981. Two authors (Professor Lord Maurice Peston and Professor Stephen Nickell) were signatories who, today, have a prominent position in public life in economics.[1] Two of the authors (Professor Philip Booth

---

1   The list of signatories and other supporting material appears in the Appendix.

and David Laws, MP) were in education at the time. The latter was educated at the leading institution promoting the theories of the 364 – Cambridge University. The former was educated at a university (the University of Durham) from which no permanent members of the economics staff were signatories. The other author, Derek Scott, had been an adviser to Denis Healey in the 1974–79 Labour government. Two of the authors (Geoffrey Wood and Patrick Minford) have chosen to republish articles that they wrote at the time of the 1981 Budget – they believe that history has justified their position and that there is little to add. Most of the other authors help us draw contemporary lessons for policy by analysing the economic evidence and political developments since 1981.

Regardless of their views on the 1981 Budget, I am sure that all the authors would agree that we need politicians who will argue their case from a position of principle and who will follow through their actions in the event of them coming under heavy fire. The Thatcher government had many battles with the intellectual elite (including over issues such as school choice, where it gave in, and over museum charges and privatisation, where it did not give in). Significant economic improvement arose in those areas of policy where the government held its nerve and stuck to the policies of liberal markets, fiscal responsibility and the pursuit of stable prices. We still await significant improvements in outcomes in the other areas, such as education and health provision where a more pragmatic course was followed.

Thus IEA Readings 60, through the accounts of so many people who have made a significant contribution to academic thinking and political life over a long period of time, has important lessons for today's politicians, not just in the field of fiscal and monetary policy, but in terms of our whole outlook on practical policy-making and implementation.

The views expressed in Readings 60 are, as in all IEA publications, those of the author and not those of the Institute (which has no corporate view), its managing trustees, Academic Advisory Council members or senior staff.

PHILIP BOOTH

Editorial and Programme Director,
Institute of Economic Affairs
Professor of Insurance and Risk Management,
Sir John Cass Business School, City University
February 2006

TABLES AND FIGURES

Were 364 Economists All Wrong?

1 WHY THE 1981 BUDGET MATTERED: THE END OF NAIVE KEYNESIANISM
Tim Congdon

The origins of naive Keynesianism

The 1981 Budget was undoubtedly a turning point in British macro-economic policy-making. It stimulated a sharp controversy about the role of fiscal policy in economic management, with 364 economists writing a letter to *The Times*[1] in protest against the raising of £4 billion in extra taxes (about 2 per cent of gross domestic product) in a recession. They warned that 'present policies will deepen the depression' and 'threaten ... social and political stability'. It is fair to say, first, that the overwhelming majority of British academic economists disapproved of the 1981 Budget and, second, that they were quite wrong in their prognoses of its consequences. This chapter discusses some of the issues in economic theory which it raised.

Until the 1930s the dominant doctrine in British public finance was that the budget should be balanced. Keynes challenged this doctrine, with many authorities citing his classic work – *The General Theory of Employment, Interest and Money* – as the rationale for discretionary fiscal policy (i.e. the deliberate unbalancing of the budget, with deficits in recessions and surpluses in booms). In fact, the remarks on fiscal policy in *The*

---

1   The letter, the signatories and associated documents are reproduced in the Appendix.

General Theory were perfunctory. The case for discretionary fiscal policy was made more explicitly in two articles on 'Paying for the War' in *The Times* on 14 and 15 November 1939.[2] These articles were a response to an unusual and very specific macroeconomic problem, the need to switch resources from peacetime uses to wartime production, but their influence was long lasting. They assumed an approach to macroeconomic analysis in which – given the present level of incomes – the sum of potential expenditures could be compared with the value of output at current prices. If potential expenditures exceeded the value of output, inflation was likely. In the 1939 articles Keynes noted that equilibrium could be restored by 'three genuine ways' and 'two pseudo-remedies'. After rejecting the pseudo-remedies (rationing and anti-profiteering), Keynes focused on the three 'genuine' answers – inflation, taxation and deferred savings. He opposed inflation, and recommended taxation and deferred savings to eliminate excess demand.

Keynes's thinking persuaded the Treasury. According to Dow, one of the UK's leading Keynesian economists in the second half of the twentieth century, writing in 1964, 'Since 1941 almost all adjustments to the total level of taxation have been made with the object of reducing excess demand or of repairing a deficiency.'[3] The remarks in the two articles in *The Times* were elaborated in a

2   The articles are reproduced on pp. 41–51 of Donald Moggridge (ed.), *The Collected Writings of John Maynard Keynes*, vol. XXII, *Activities 1939–45: Internal War Finance*, London and Basingstoke: Macmillan, for the Royal Economic Society, 1978.

3   J. C. R. [Christopher] Dow, *The Management of the British Economy 1945–60*, Cambridge: Cambridge University Press, 1964, p. 178. Dow has a high reputation in some circles. Peter Jay, the former economics editor of the BBC, has referred to 'the learned Dow' and described his book on *Major Recessions* as 'magisterial' (Jay, *The Wealth of Man*, New York: Public Affairs, 2000, p. 238).

theory of national income determination which took hold in the textbooks of the 1950s and 1960s. Quoting from Dow again (this time from a book on *Major Recessions* published in 1998):

> Interpretation of events cannot depend on unstructured observation, but has to be based on assumptions ... about the causal structure of the economy ... Total demand is defined in terms of real final expenditure; its level (in the absence of shocks) is determined by previous income; its result is output, in the course of producing which income is generated; income in turn goes to determine demand in the subsequent period.[4]

In short, income determines expenditures which determine income and output which determine expenditures which determine income and output and so on, as if in a never-ending circle. The circular flow of incomes and expenditure is conceived here as being between passive private sector agents with no way of adding to or subtracting from incomes from one period to the next, and without the inclination to vary the proportion of incomes that are spent. According to Dow's statement, the flow of private sector expenditures would proceed indefinitely at the same level, were it not for 'shocks'.

The textbooks did, however, allow for additions to or subtractions from the circular flow by an active, well-intentioned and appropriately advised government. If the state itself spent above or beneath its tax revenue (i.e. it ran a budget deficit or surplus), it could add to or subtract from the circular flow.[5] The

---

4 Christopher Dow, *Major Recessions: Britain and the World 1920–95*, Oxford: Oxford University Press, 1998, p. 38.

5 The other recognised source of demand injections and withdrawals was the rest of the world, via the balance of payments.

notion of a circular flow of income, and the related idea of the income–expenditure model of the economy (which was adopted in econometric forecasting in the late 1960s and 1970s), therefore made fiscal policy the favourite weapon in the macroeconomic armoury. If all went well, the fiscal additions to and subtractions from the circular flow could be designed to keep the economy at full employment with price stability (or, at any rate, acceptably low inflation). The official judgement on the size of these additions and subtractions, announced with accompanying political theatre every year in the Budget, was taken to be of great significance. For economists brought up to believe that the income–expenditure model was an accurate description of 'how the economy worked' (and that included probably over 90 per cent of the UK's university economists at the time), the 1981 Budget was shockingly inept. They saw it as withdrawing demand in any economy where expenditure was weak and unemployment rising, and so as being totally misguided.

The circular flow of income is a useful teaching aid and is understandably popular in university macroeconomics courses. It is, however, a primitive and incomplete account of national income determination. If this is 'Keynesianism', it is 'naive Keynesianism'. Substantial amendments are needed to bring the story closer to the truth – and indeed to the authentic Keynes of the major works.

Problems with naive Keynesianism

At the level of the individual private sector agent, it is incorrect to state that income and expenditure are the same in every period, for two reasons. The first is simple. As agents hold money balances, they can spend above income in any given period by running down these balances. (Of course, if they spend beneath income, they add to their money holdings.) The second is more troublesome. The motive of Keynesian analysis is to determine national expenditure and income, in order to fix the level of employment. So the relevant 'expenditures' are those that lead to output *in the current period* and so necessitate employment. It is evident that expenditure on existing assets – such as houses that were built decades ago, ships after they have been launched, antiques inherited from previous generations and so on – does not result in more employment: the assets have been made *in past periods* and do not need to be made again. But purchases and sales of assets, and of financial securities that establish claims to assets, are on an enormous scale. As with money, an individual agent can spend above income in any given period by selling an asset and spending the proceeds, or spend beneath income by purchasing an asset out of savings from current income. Goods can be bought with money arising from the sale of assets and assets can be bought with money arising from the sale of goods.

At the aggregate level, the situation becomes even more complicated. Suppose, to ease the exposition, that an economy has no assets. If the amount of money is given for the economy as a whole, decisions by individual agents to run down or build up their money balances cannot alter the aggregate amount of money. Even in this asset-less economy, however, the amount of spending can vary between periods if the velocity of circulation of money changes. Of course, if the amount of money increases or declines from one period to the next, that also allows the level of expenditures to change while the velocity of circulation remains constant.[6]

Now remove the assumption of an asset-less economy. Money is used in two types of transaction. The first type relates to current expenditure (i.e. expenditure that contributes to 'aggregate demand'), output and employment, and belongs to the circular flow; the second type relates to expenditure on existing assets. This second type leads to asset redispositions and, typically, to changes in asset ownership. Total transactions consist of both transactions in the circular flow *and transactions in assets*. It should be noted that this distinction is not new. In fact, it was made by Keynes in his *Treatise on Money*, which was published in 1930 before *The General Theory*. To adopt his terms, 'deposits' (i.e. money) are used partly in 'industry' and partly in 'finance'. The 'industrial circulation' was concerned with 'maintaining the normal process of current output, distribution and exchange, and paying the factors of production their incomes'; the 'financial circulation', on the other hand, was involved with 'holding and exchanging existing titles to wealth, including stock exchange and money market transactions' and even 'speculation'.[7, 8]

How are these ideas to be put to analytical use? It is imme-

---

6   As usual in discussions of these concepts, the question of the timing of the receipt of 'income' and the disbursal of 'expenditure' is left a little vague. The income—expenditure story is most plausible if people have nothing (i.e. neither money nor assets) at the end of a period, and receive their income at the beginning of a period and have spent it all by the same period's end. In other words, the story is easiest to tell about an economy without private property of any kind.

7   Donald Moggridge and Elizabeth Johnson (eds), *Collected Writings of Keynes*, vol. V, *A Treatise on Money: 1. The Pure Theory of Money*, London and Basingstoke: Macmillan, 1971 (1st edn 1930), p. 217.

8   Of course, in the real world the same sum of money may be used in a transaction in goods one day and a transaction in assets the next. Money circulates endlessly. The distinction between the industrial and financial circulations – like any distinction relating to something as fluid as money – is to that degree artificial.

diately clear that, with the quantity of money given, the value of aggregate demand can change for two reasons. First, the velocity of circulation of money in total transactions may alter, with the relative size of Keynes's industrial and financial circulations constant. Second, the velocity of circulation of money in total transactions may stay the same, but the relative size of the industrial and financial circulations could change. It should be unnecessary to add that, if the quantity of money increases or decreases between periods, that introduces yet another potential source of disturbance.

In short, once the economy is allowed to have money and assets, the idea of a simple period-after-period equivalence of income and expenditure becomes implausible. The circular flow of income and expenditure would remain a valid description of the economy if the following were constant:

1   the quantity of money;
2   the velocity of money in total transactions; and
3   the proportion of transactions in the circular flow to total transactions (or, in Keynes's terminology in *The Treatise on Money*, the ratio between the industrial circulation and the industrial and financial circulations combined).

A brief glance at the real world shows that the quantity, the velocity and the uses of money are changing all the time. Some economists, however, brush these matters to one side and stick to a simple income–expenditure model when they interpret the real world. A common short cut is to take expenditures as being determined in naive Keynesian fashion and to claim that the quantity of money then adjusts to the level of expenditures.

To quote from Dow again, 'Change in nominal GDP [i.e. gross domestic product] determines change in broad money. Money is thus not the driving force in the economy, but rather the residuary determinant [*sic*].'[9]

But Dow is simply wrong. Banks are forever expanding and contracting their balance sheets for reasons that have nothing whatever to do with the recent or current levels of nominal GDP. For example, when banks lend to customers to finance the purchase of old houses, land and long-established companies (i.e. to finance the purchase of existing assets), they add to the quantity of money, but their activities do not in the first instance impinge on the industrial circulation. They have no immediate and direct effect on national income or expenditure. Nevertheless, agents have to reshuffle their money holdings and portfolios – in a second, third or further round of transactions – so that the extra money is again in balance with their wealth and current expenditure. The vital principle becomes that national income *and the value of assets* are in equilibrium, and so incomes and expenditure are likely to remain the same period after period, only when the demand to hold money balances is equal to the supply of such balances (i.e. to the quantity of money) at the end of each and every period, and when the quantity of money is constant. More briefly, national income is in equilibrium only when 'monetary equilibrium' also prevails. After all, it was Keynes himself who said: '... incomes and prices necessarily change until the aggregate of the amounts of money which individuals choose to hold at the new level of incomes and prices ... has come to equality with

---

9   Dow, *Major Recessions*, p. 39. Given the context, Dow must have meant 'determinand', not 'determinant'.

the amount of money created by the banking system. That ... is the fundamental proposition of monetary theory'.[10]

On this view changes in the quantity of money – particularly big changes in the quantity of money – shatter the cosy equivalence of income and expenditure which is the kernel of naive Keynesianism. Indeed, a sudden sharp acceleration in the rate of money supply growth might create a severe 'monetary disequilibrium', and initiate adjustment processes in which first asset prices and later the prices of goods and services would have to change.[11] A 25 per cent jump in the quantity of money would – with some technical caveats – increase the equilibrium nominal values of both national income *and national wealth* also by 25 per cent. One interesting possibility cannot be excluded. It might be that – in the period of transition from the old equilibrium to the new – some asset prices need to rise by more than 25 per cent, in order to stimulate excess demand in goods markets and motivate the required 25 per cent rise in national income At any rate, in any comprehensive account of the determination of national income economists must have a theory of money-holding behaviour, and this theory has to recognise that money is only one part of a larger portfolio of assets.

10 Moggridge and Johnson (eds), *Collected Writings of Keynes*, vol. VII, *The General Theory*, pp. 84–5. Note that – in this quotation – the word 'prices' referred to the prices of *securities*, not of goods and services.

11 These processes are discussed in more detail in the author's *Money and Asset Prices in Boom and Bust* (London: Institute of Economic Affairs, 2005). It seems that – after a big change in the amount of money – asset prices change with a shorter lag and by larger percentages than the prices of goods and services. The explanation for this undoubted pattern is important to the analysis of real-world business cycles.

Naive Keynesianism and the 1981 Budget

All this may seem a long way from the 1981 Budget. It is there-fore now time to bring the discussion back to the contemporary context by discussing the values of income, money, assets and related variables in Britain at the time. The UK's money GDP in 1980 and 1981 was about £215 billion and £233 billion respectively. The gross wealth of the personal sector at the end of 1980 was estimated at £658 billion, split between £461 billion of physical assets (mostly houses) and £283 billion of financial assets, and offset by £86 billion of debt to leave net wealth at £658 billion. Total national wealth – including public sector and corporate assets – was nearer £1,100 billion. At the end of 1980 the quantity of money, on the very broad M4 measure which included building society deposits, was worth slightly above £130 billion, while sterling M3 (the subject of the official money targets then in force) was £68.5 billion. The value of all transactions – including all cheque and other clearings between the banks – in 1980 was over £4,000 billion.

A number of comments need to be made straight away about these numbers. Two features are striking. First, the value of all transactions was a very high multiple of money GDP (or 'national income'). Roughly speaking, total transactions were about twenty times as large as national income. Second, wealth was a high multiple of money GDP. To say that wealth was five times national income would be broadly correct, although the precise multiple depends on the valuation conventions adopted. Most wealth was owned by the personal sector, even though some of it was held indirectly via financial products of various kinds. Housing was the personal sector's principal asset.

It is obvious that the national income and expenditure, the

central actors in the naive Keynesians' circular flow, took bit parts in the wider drama of total transactions. To repeat, national income was somewhat more than £200 billion, while total transactions exceeded £4,000 billion. Plainly, the majority of the transactions were not in goods and services, but in assets. In terms of size, the financial circulation dominated the industrial circulation. The preponderance of asset transactions was partly due to the second salient feature, that the value of national wealth was five times that of national income. The value of turnover on the London Stock Exchange in 1980 was £196.3 billion, not much less than GDP, while the value of turnover in gilt-edged securities was over £150 billion. In addition, there were transactions in foreign exchange, in unquoted companies and small businesses, in houses, commercial property and land, and in such items as antiques, second-hand cars and personal chattels.

How does this bear on the debate about the 1981 Budget? The 1980 Budget had proposed a medium-term financial strategy (MTFS) for both the budget deficit (defined in terms of the public sector borrowing requirement or PSBR) as a percentage of GDP and money supply growth. Targets for both these variables had been set for the financial years up to and including 1983/84. The target for 1981/82 in the 1980 Budget was 3 per cent of GDP. In practice the PSBR in the closing months of 1980 proved much higher than expected and the projections in early 1981 were that, on unchanged policies, the PSBR/GDP ratio in 1981/82 would be over 5 per cent. The government wanted to restore the credibility of the MTFS. It therefore announced, in the 1981 Budget, tax increases and other measures that would cut the PSBR/GDP ratio in 1981/82 by about 2 per cent of GDP (i.e. by about £4 billion). This tightening of fiscal policy at a time of recession was

Table 1 **Value of the main items in the UK personal sector's wealth, 1979–82**

All values in £m

	1979	1980	1981	1982
Notes and coin	7,717	8,307	8,837	9,153
Bank deposits	36,210	43,188	47,662	51,685
Building society deposits	42,442	49,617	56,699	66,993
All monetary assets	86,369	101,112	113,198	127,831
Dwellings	276,600	313,200	323,700	345,900
Equity in life assurance pension funds	37,000	49,000	57,000	75,000
UK ordinary shares	31,389	36,482	38,297	45,035
Three leading assets classes combined	344,989	398,682	418,997	465,935
Net wealth	580,529	657,903	696,909	776,754

Source: Financial Statistics, London: HMSO, February 1984, Table S12, p. 140

what provoked the letter to *The Times* from the 364 economists. For economists who believed in naive Keynesianism and the income–expenditure model, a demand withdrawal of 2 per cent of GDP implied that over the year or so from March 1981 national expenditure and income would be at least 2 per cent lower than would otherwise be the case. (Some of them might appeal to the multiplier concept, also developed in Keynesian textbooks, to say that the adverse impact on demand would be 2 per cent plus something extra because of supposed 'multiplier effects'.)

But hold on. As the last few paragraphs have shown, the total annual value of transactions in Britain at the time of the 1981 Budget was over £4,000 billion. The £4 billion tax increase might seem quite big relative to national income and expenditure, but it was a fleabite – a mere 0.1 per cent – of total transactions. Given that national wealth is about five times national income, the impact of changes in national wealth on expenditure has to be brought into the discussion. As it happened, the 1981 Budget was accompanied by a reduction in interest rates, with the Bank of England's Minimum Lending Rate falling from 14 per cent to 12 per cent. This cut followed an earlier one, from 16 per cent to 14 per cent, on 25 November 1980. The value of the UK housing stock and quoted equity market was rising throughout the period, partly because of rather high money growth and (from the autumn of 1980 onwards) the easing of monetary policy. Over the three years to end-1982 the value of the personal sector's money holdings advanced by over £40 billion and the value of the three largest other items in its wealth (dwellings, equity in life assurance and pension funds, and directly owned 'UK ordinary shares') increased by more than £120 billion and of its net wealth by almost £200 billion; see Table 1. These numbers are an order of magnitude larger than the £4 billion tax increase in the 1981 Budget. Should anyone be surprised that the Budget was not followed by a deepening of 'the depression' or by an erosion of 'the industrial base of our economy' which would 'threaten its social and political stability'?

After the 1981 Budget

With a delightful irony, the recovery in the economy began almost immediately after the letter from the 364 appeared in *The Times*. The chart above shows the annualised growth of domestic demand, in real terms, in two-quarter periods from the start of the Conservative government in mid-1979 to the end of 1984. In

Figure 1   **Annualised growth in domestic expenditure, in real terms, in two-quarter periods ending in quarter specified**
%

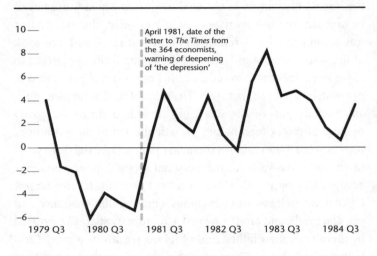

every two-quarter period from mid-1979 to the first quarter of 1981 domestic demand fell in real terms; in every two-quarter period over the five years from quarter one of 1981 domestic demand rose in real terms (with two minor exceptions). From mid-1979 to quarter one of 1981 the compound annualised rate of fall in domestic demand was 3.8 per cent; in the five years from quarter one of 1981 the compound annual rate of increase in domestic demand was 3.3 per cent. The warnings of a deepening of the depression were not just wrong, but hopelessly so.

Relative importance of monetary and fiscal policy

Of course, there is much more to be said about the behaviour of the economy in this period. A naive Keynesian might ask why – if asset prices were gaining ground in 1980 and 1981 – a recession had occurred at all. While the causes of the 1980 recession are complex, the dominant consideration was plainly the very high level of interest rates. Minimum Lending Rate (then the name for the interest rate on which the Bank of England operated) had been raised to 17 per cent on 30 November 1979 and the average level of clearing bank base rates in 1980 was over 16 per cent. This had discouraged demand by familiar Keynesian mechanisms (i.e. it had deterred some investment). But monetary forces had also been at work. Dear money had caused money supply growth to be lower than would otherwise have been the case, and encouraged people and companies to hold a higher ratio of interest-bearing money balances to their expenditure. Although money supply growth had been higher than targeted, real money balances had in fact been squeezed. The precise strength of these different 'Keynesian' and 'monetary' influences on demand is difficult to disentangle.

An annex to this chapter derives estimates of the change in the cyclically adjusted public sector financial deficit (PSFD), as a percentage of GDP, and the change in real broad money balances on an annual basis from 1949 to 2004. The change in the PSFD/GDP ratio is usually regarded as a satisfactory summary measure of fiscal policy. The change in real domestic demand was then regressed on the two variables over four periods, the whole period (1949–2004) and three sub-periods (1949–64, usually regarded as the heyday of 'the Keynesian revolution', 1965–80 and 1981–2004). The resulting equation for fiscal policy over the whole 1949–2004 period was poor, although not totally disastrous, with an r-squared of 0.11 and a t-statistic on the regression coefficient of 2.56 (i.e. slightly less than the value of 3 usually thought necessary for a significant relationship). The equation for real broad money was better. It had an r-squared of 0.31 and a t-statistic on the regression coefficient of 4.98. In the 1981–2004 period, however, no relationship whatever obtained between the change in domestic demand and fiscal policy, whereas monetary policy – as measured by the change in real broad money – still seemed to be working. While this exercise is primitive, it suggests that the naive Keynesian faith in fiscal policy in 1981 was mistaken. By contrast, the role of the 'real balance effect' – routinely dismissed by Keynesians as virtually irrelevant to the determination of demand – justifies much more investigation.

The debate between Congdon and Hahn

The author of this chapter wrote an article in *The Times* on 14 July 1983, under the title 'How 364 economists can be wrong – with the figures to prove it'. It argued that the thinking behind the MTFS was 'that the economy had in-built mechanisms which would sooner or later lead to improved business conditions'. It also pointed out that economies had grown, admittedly with cyclical fluctuations, for centuries before 'the invention of fiscal fine tuning, demand reflation and the rest of the Keynesian toolkit'. One key sentence was: 'if we are to understand how the economy might recover without government stimulus today, we should look at wealth and credit'. Particular attention was paid to the housing market and mortgage credit, since 'borrowing for house purchase is the biggest financial transaction most people undertake'. Data in an accompanying table showed that mortgage credit had more than doubled from £6,590 million in 1979 to £13,795 million in 1982.

A reply appeared in the letters column of *The Times* on 29 July from Frank Hahn, one of the two economics professors at the University of Cambridge who had initiated the original letter criticising the 1981 Budget. Hahn deserves two cheers because he did at least try to defend the 1981 letter, whereas most of the 364 have clammed up.[12] Its opening paragraph was lively and polemical, and may be recalled over twenty years later:

> Suppose 364 doctors stated that there is 'no basis in medical theory or supporting evidence' that a man with an infection will be cured by the administration of toad's liver. Suppose, none the less, that the man is given toad's liver and shows signs of recovery. Mr Congdon (July 14) wants us to conclude that the doctors were wrong. This is slightly unfair since Mr Congdon provides a 'theory' of how toad's liver may do good to the patient.

It went on to claim that the recovery in the economy (which Hahn did not dispute) could be explained in 'entirely Keynesian' terms, by the fall in interest rates and its impact on consumer spending.[13]

---

12 The author knows a few of them – with later careers of great public prominence – who would prefer not to be reminded that they signed it.

13 Hahn made an attempt at self-justification by claiming that 'the monetarists' deny that an injection of newly printed money can boost demand because inflation expectations would deteriorate and 'nothing "real" will be changed'. But this is to equate 'monetarism' with the New Classical Economics of Lucas, Barro, Sargent and others. It is now widely recognised that these are distinct schools of economics. (See, for example, K. D. Hoover, 'Two types of monetarism', *Journal of Economic Literature*, vol. 22, 1984, pp. 58–76.) Hahn's letter ended with a sneer: 'Mr Congdon's understanding of either side of the argument [by which

The trouble here is twofold. First, if Hahn had always believed that a fall in interest rates could rescue the economy, why did he help organise the letter from the 364? It is uncontroversial both that a decline in interest rates ought to stimulate demand and that the 1981 Budget was intended to facilitate a reduction in interest rates. Presumably Hahn's concern was about relative magnitudes. He thought that the £4 billion of supposed 'demand withdrawal' announced in the Budget could not be offset by the positive effect on demand of the drop in interest rates and the rise in asset values. If so, he may have shared a characteristic of Cambridge macroeconomic thinking in the immediate post-war decades, that demand is interest-inelastic and that policy-makers should instead rely on fiscal measures.[14] One purpose of this author's article on 14 July 1983 was to show that the housing market was highly responsive to interest rates and that pessimism about the economy's in-built recovery mechanisms was misplaced.[15]

---

he presumably meant either the Keynesian or monetarist side] seems very insecure.'

14 'Elasticity pessimism', i.e. a belief that behaviour did not respond to price signals, was common among British economists in the first twenty or thirty years after the Second World War. Investment was thought to be unresponsive to interest rates, while exports and imports were held to be impervious to changes in the exchange rate. Leijonhufvud has outlined one 'familiar type of argument' as the claim that 'The interest-elasticity of investment is for various reasons quite low. Hence, monetary policy is not a very useful stabilization instrument'. Hahn and the 364 may have been thinking on these lines. Leijonhufvud says that 'the dogma' of the interest-inelasticity of investment originated in Oxford, with surveys of businessmen carried out in 1938, not in Cambridge. (Axel Leijonhufvud, *On Keynesian Economics and the Economics of Keynes*, New York: Oxford University Press, 1968, p. 405.) But it was still widely held in Cambridge and other British universities in the 1970s and even in the 1980s.

15 Before the July 1983 article in *The Times* the author had proposed the concept of 'mortgage equity withdrawal' in a joint paper with Paul Turnbull. (See 'Introducing the concept of "equity withdrawal"', in Tim Congdon, *Reflections on Monetarism*, Aldershot and Brookfield, VT: Edward Elgar, for the Institute of Economic

Second, and much more fundamentally, Hahn's polemics concealed the deeply unsatisfactory state of Cambridge and indeed British macroeconomics. To simplify greatly but not in a misleading way, part of Keynes's contribution to economic thinking had been to propose a new theory of national income determination. In that theory, national income was equal to national expenditure and expenditure was a multiple of so-called 'autonomous expenditure' (i.e. investment and government spending). Dow's recapitulation of the circular flow of incomes and expenditure in *Major Recessions* was of course very much in this tradition. But Keynes fully recognised that the new theory was a supplement to an existing theory, 'the monetary theory'. As already explained, when money and assets are introduced into the economy, the equilibrium relationship between them and expenditure has inevitably to be part of the story. Keynes did not intend that the new theory should replace the old theory.

The failings of British academic economists and their role in boom and bust

In a celebrated paper written in 1937, as a review article on Keynes's *General Theory*, Hicks had tried to reconcile the two

Affairs, pp. 274–87, based on a paper of 4 June 1982 for the stockbroking firm of L. Messel & Co., 'The coming boom in housing credit'.) Dozens of articles have subsequently been written about 'mortgage equity withdrawal' and its influence on personal expenditure, and the Bank of England regularly prepares estimates of its size. To economists spoon-fed at university on the circular flow of income and the income–expenditure model (in which, as explained, assets do not affect expenditure), mortgage equity withdrawal was a striking idea. It showed how people whose only significant asset was a house (which is of course rather illiquid) could tap into the equity (often boosted in the Britain of the early 1980s by house price inflation) by borrowing.

theories in a model (the so-called IS-LM model) where national income was a multiple of investment and investment was equal to savings (i.e. the IS curve was thus defined), and where national income and the interest rate were at levels that equilibrated the demand for money with the supply (i.e. the LM curve was also thus defined). Full equilibrium, with the determination of both interest rates and national income, was achieved by the intersection of the two curves. But in practice most British economists had found the monetary side of the story complicated and confusing, and sidestepped the difficulties by the sort of procedures adopted in Dow's *Major Recessions*. Like Dow, they fixed national income from their income–expenditure model and assumed that the quantity of money adjusted passively (or, in the jargon, 'endogenously'). The quantity of money could then have no causal role in the economy. The LM part of the IS-LM model, and the possibility that asset prices and incomes might have to change to keep the demand to hold money (i.e. 'liquidity preferences' or L) in line with 'the amount of money created by the banking system' (i.e. M), was suppressed. What Keynes deemed in *The General Theory* 'the fundamental proposition of monetary theory' had disappeared from view.[16]

16 Note that monetary equilibrium could refer to
   i   the equivalence of the demand for base money with the supply of base money, or
   ii   the equivalence of the demand for narrow money with the supply of narrow money, or
   iii the equivalence of the demand for a broad money measure with the supply of broad money, or
   iv   the simultaneous equivalence of the demand for all money measures with the supply of all such measures.

The 'which aggregate?' debate will not go away. The chaos in the subject helps to explain why so many economists have dropped money from their analytical purview.

The message of the letter from the 364 was that British academic economists could not see national income determination in monetary terms. They were angry because the Thatcher government had adopted monetary targets to defeat inflation and subordinated fiscal policy to these targets, and because monetary targets made sense only if their pet theory were wrong and the monetary theory of national income determination were correct. In retrospect, it is clear that the 364 had a very poor understanding of the forces determining output, employment and the price level. The LM part of the story mattered then (as it matters now), but the 364 could not see the connections between money growth and macroeconomic outcomes. Although policy-making has improved dramatically since the 1970s and 1980s, a fair comment is that British economists are still uncomfortable with monetary analysis. No one knows whether that discomfort will lead through mistaken policy decisions to another boom–bust cycle. But it can be argued that the 1981 letter to *The Times* was part of a wider assault on money supply targeting which led to the abandonment of broad money targets in 1985 and 1986. The sequel was the disastrous Lawson boom and ERM bust of the 1985–92 period. That boom–bust cycle can therefore be blamed on British economists' poor knowledge of monetary economics; it reflected, in other words, 'a great vacuum in intellectual understanding'.[17] In that sense the last big boom–bust cycle was the revenge of the 364 on the Thatcher government.

---

17   Congdon, *Reflections*, p. 252.

Conclusion: the end of naive Keynesianism

At any rate, the 1981 Budget was the end of naive Keynesianism. It is now over 25 years since British governments renounced the annual adjustment of fiscal policy to manage demand. In that 25-year period fiscal policy has been subordinate either to monetary policy or to rather vague requirements of 'prudence'. In decisions on the size of the budget deficit, governments have respected the aim of keeping public debt under control over a medium-term timeframe. The central theme of macroeconomic policy-making today is instead the discretionary adjustment of a short-term interest rate by an independent Bank of England to keep demand growing in such a way that actual output is, as far as possible, equal to trend output (i.e. the output gap is zero). Professor Hahn – and as many of the 364 who are still alive and prepared to put their heads above the parapet – might regard the disappearance of fiscal fine tuning and the apotheosis of interest-rate setting as a diet of 'toad's liver'. Someone should tell them that the patient has lapped it up. The British economy has been more stable over the last twelve years than in any previous period of comparable length. Policy-makers do not pay all that much attention to fiscal policy in their macroeconomic prognoses, although – depressingly – it is still possible to come across textbooks that proclaim the virtues of fiscal policy and its ability to manage demand.[18]

---

18 For example, Ben Bernanke and Robert Frank's textbook *Principles of Macroeconomics*, New York: Irwin/McGraw-Hill, 2nd edn, 2003, contains an account of national income determination and the efficacy of fiscal action which could have been lifted, in its entirety, from a similar textbook of the 1950s. Bernanke was professor of economics at Princeton University, a university widely regarded as in the vanguard of macroeconomic thought, when the textbook was published. Now – as chairman of the board of governors of the USA's Federal Reserve – he holds the most important position in monetary policy-making in the world.

As foreshadowed by the author's article in *The Times* in July 1983, the relationship between interest rates and the housing market has become a more central part of macroeconomic analysis than the supposed impact of changes in the budget deficit in adding to or subtracting from the circular flow of income and expenditure. Nowadays the Bank of England is particularly active in research on the housing market.[19] Much attention is paid to the rate of house price inflation (or deflation), because the change in the price of this asset is thought to have a major influence on consumer spending. But houses are only one asset class. In truth the level and rate of change of all asset prices matter. A key point has now to be reiterated: any plausible theory of money-holding behaviour has to recognise that money is only one part of a larger portfolio of assets. If a number of conditions are met (and over long runs they are met, more or less, in most economies), a 1 per cent change in the rate of money supply growth is associated with a 1 per cent increase in the equilibrium rate of change of both nominal national income *and the value of national wealth*. Moreover, national wealth is typically a high multiple of national income. It follows that a sudden acceleration in the rate of money supply growth (of the kind seen in the early phases of the two great boom–bust cycles of the early 1970s and late 1980s) leads to outbreaks of asset price inflation. Big leaps in asset prices cause people and companies to sell assets, and to buy more goods and services, disrupting the smooth flows of incomes and expenditure hypothesised in the naive Keynesian stories. Because the value of

---

19   In the 1970s the Bank of England's *Quarterly Bulletin* did not include a single arti-
cle on the housing market. In the three years to the summer of 2005 the *Quarterly Bulletin* carried seven articles and two speeches by the members of the Monetary Policy Committee which related specifically to the housing market.

all assets combined is so much higher than the value of national income, the circular income–expenditure flow is a thoroughly misleading way of thinking about the determination of economic activity.

The macroeconomic effects of the £4 billion tax increase in the 1981 Budget were smothered by the much larger and more powerful macroeconomic effects of changes in monetary policy. No doubt the naive Keynesian would complain that this is to compare apples and pears, as hypothetical changes in asset values and their impact on expenditure are a long way from the readily quantified and easily forecast impact of budgetary measures. But that would be to duck the main question. As the sequel to the 1981 Budget showed, the naive Keynesians are kidding themselves if they think either that the economy is adequately described by the income–expenditure model or that the impact of budgetary measures on the economy is easy to forecast: as the author argued in a series of articles in *The Times* in the mid-1970s on 'crowding out', the effect of such measures depends heavily on how they are financed and, specifically, on whether they lead to extra money creation.[20] The majority of British economists, however, do not think that the income–expenditure model has been discredited by the sequel to the 1981 Budget. For example, the Bank of England's macro-econometric model – which purportedly is the starting point in its forecasting exercises – remains a large-scale elaboration of an income–expenditure model in which money is, to use the phrase that Dow presumably intended, a 'residuary determinand'.[21] Macroeconomics must embrace monetary economics,

---

20 See, for example, Tim Congdon, 'The futility of deficit financing as a cure for recession', *The Times*, 23 October 1975.

21 See The Bank of England Quarterly Model. London: Bank of England, 2005, *passim*.

and integrate the ideas of monetary and portfolio equilibria (and disequilibria) in the theory of national income determination if it is to come closer to reality.

It is ironic that the two instigators of the 1981 letter thought themselves to be protecting the 'Keynesian' position in British policy-making and to be attacking 'the monetarists'.[22] As this chapter has shown, Keynes's writings – or at any rate his book-length writings – are replete with references to banks, deposits,

22 The two instigators were Professor Robert Neild and Professor Frank Hahn. Neild's subsequent interests were in peace studies and corruption in public life. (He has also written a history of the oyster in England and France.) As far as the author can determine, he dropped macroeconomics at some point in the 1980s. Hahn's position is more interesting and, in the author's opinion, more puzzling. He has written numerous academic papers on money (and money-related issues) in general equilibrium theory, brought together in Frank Hahn, *Equilibrium and Macroeconomics*, Oxford: Basil Blackwell, 1984. Most of the papers in this book were concerned with rarefied topics, such as the existence, stability and optimality of differently specified general equilibria. Four of the papers, however (numbered 12 to 15), were more or less directly polemical exercises whose target was 'monetarism' or, at any rate, what Hahn took to be 'monetarism'. They cannot be summarised here for reasons of space, but a salient feature of all the papers was the lack of references to real-world institutions, behaviours and magnitudes. Following Keynes, this author has argued – in the current paper and elsewhere – that a discussion of the determination of national income must be, to a large extent, a discussion of the role of money in portfolios. In a 1980 paper on 'Monetarism and economic theory' Hahn cited a number of recondite papers before seeing in 'recent macroliterature' two elements 'that Keynesians have for long ignored'. One was the portfolio consequences of budget deficits and the other 'wealth effects' (*Equilibrium and Macroeconomics*, p. 299). Given that, might one ask – after all these years – why Hahn should have been so sarcastic about the author's 1983 article in *The Times*, and its concern with mortgage credit, houses and wealth? And might one also ask whether he really believes (as apparently he did in 1980 and perhaps as he continued to do when he orchestrated the 1981 letter to *The Times*) that the government should make 'the rate of change of the money stock proportional to the difference between actual unemployment and half a million unemployed' (*Equilibrium and Macroeconomics*, p. 305)? Is that the sort of policy which – on a considered analysis – would have led to the macroeconomic stability the UK has enjoyed since 1992?

portfolios, bond prices and suchlike. No one can say whether he would have approved of the 1981 letter, but it is pretty definite that he would not have based a macroeconomic forecast purely on fiscal variables. The concepts of the industrial and financial circulations were proposed in the *Treatise* in 1930. They are building blocks in a more complete and powerful theory of national income determination than the simplistic income–expenditure notions advanced in the 'Paying for the War' articles of November 1939. If the Keynesians had paid more attention to what Keynes had said in his great works rather than in his journalism, and if they had been rather more sophisticated in their comments on money and wealth, they might not have been so embarrassingly wrong about the 1981 Budget.

Annex: Does naive fiscalism or naive monetarism fit the UK data better?

Doubts have been raised about the validity of the monetary theory of national income determination, with some of the sceptics adopting high-powered econometrics to make their point. In 1983 Hendry and Ericsson published a well-known critique of the methodology used in Friedman and Schwartz's *Monetary Trends in the United States and the United Kingdom.*[23] Relatively little work has been directed at assessing the empirical validity of the proposition that changes in domestic demand are heavily, or perhaps even predominantly, influenced by changes in the budget deficit

23   David Hendry and N. R. Ericsson, 'Assertion without empirical basis: an econometric appraisal of *Monetary Trends in the United States and United Kingdom*, by Milton Friedman and Anna Schwartz', in Bank of England Panel of Economic Consultants, *Monetary Trends in the United Kingdom*, Panel paper no. 22, October 1983, pp. 45–101.

(which might be called 'the fiscalist [or naive Keynesian] theory of national income determination'). The purpose of this annex is to compare simple formulations of the fiscal and monetary theories of national income determination. In view of British economists' inclination to downplay or even to dismiss the monetary theory (on the grounds that 'it does not stand up to the facts'), and then to advocate changes in the budget deficit as an appropriate macroeconomic therapy, an exercise on these lines is needed. Series were obtained over the 1948–2004 period for

- the cyclically adjusted ratio of the pubic sector financial deficit (PSFD) to GDP, and hence for the change in the ratio from 1949;
- the change in real broad money, using the M4 measure of money adjusted by the increase in the deflator for GDP at market prices (the M4 data after 1964 were taken from the official Office for National Statistics website; the M4 data before 1964 used a series prepared at Lombard Street Research);[24]
- the change in real domestic demand, where the deflator for GDP at market prices was again used to obtain the real-terms numbers.

The cyclical adjustment to the PSFD data was conducted in the same way as in the author's paper 'Did Britain have a Keynesian revolution? – fiscal policy since 1941', pp. 84–115.[25, 26]

---

24 This drew on data from Forrest Capie and Alan Webber, *A Monetary History of the United Kingdom, 1870–1982*, vol. 1, London: Allen & Unwin, 1985.

25 See John Maloney (ed.), *Debt and Deficits*, Cheltenham and Northampton, ME: Edward Elgar, 1998.

26 For the years 1963/64 to 1986/87 the author's numbers for the cyclically adjusted

The change in real domestic demand was regressed against, first, the change in the cyclically adjusted PSFD/GDP ratio (to test a naive fiscalist hypothesis) and, second, the change in real M4 (to test a naive monetarist hypothesis) for four periods, 1949–2004 as a whole, 1949–64 (i.e. the heyday of 'the Keynesian revolution'), 1965–80 (the period when the Keynesian dominance in policy thinking was being eroded) and 1981–2004 (the period when medium-term fiscal rules were adopted, initially because of 'monetarism', but later because of Mr Gordon Brown's 'prudence'). The results are given in the following box.

1 **The whole 1949–2004 period**

Naive fiscalism

Change in real domestic demand (per cent p.a.) = 2.61 + 0.56 change in PSFD/GDP ratio (per cent of GDP, in year in question)

$R^2 = 0.11$

t statistic on regression coefficient = 2.56

Naive monetarism

Change in real domestic demand (per cent p.a.) = 1.74 + 0.28 change in real M4 (per cent p.a.)

$R^2 = 0.31$

t statistic on regression coefficient = 4.98

PSFD/GDP ratio are virtually identical to those given in H.M Treasury's Occasional Paper no. 4 on *Public Finances and the Cycle*, published in September 1995. The change in the cyclically adjusted public sector financial deficit is usually accepted as a satisfactory summary measure of fiscal policy. The data are available from timcongdon@btinternet.com.

2 The 1949–64 sub-period ('the Keynesian revolution')

Change in real domestic demand (per cent p.a.) = 2.68 +
0.73 change in PSFD/GDP ratio (per cent of GDP)
$R^2 = 0.19$
t statistic on regression coefficient = 1.82

Change in real domestic demand (per cent p.a.) = 2.87 +
0.34 change in real M4 (per cent p.a.)
$R^2 = 0.23$
t statistic on regression coefficient = 2.03

3 The 1965–80 sub-period (the breakdown of the Keynesian consensus)

Change in real domestic demand (per cent p.a.) = 1.96 +
0.98 change in PSFD/GDP ratio (per cent of GDP)
$R^2 = 0.35$
t statistic on regression coefficient = 2.72

Change in real domestic demand (per cent p.a.) = 1.16 +
0.37 change in real M4 (per cent p.a.)
$R^2 = 0.66$
t statistic on regression coefficient = 5.20

4 The 1981–2004 sub-period (the period of medium-term fiscal rules)

Change in real domestic demand (per cent p.a.) = 2.92 –
0.06 change in PSFD/GDP ratio (per cent of GDP)
$R^2 = 0.001$
t statistic on regression coefficient = –0.16

Change in real domestic demand (per cent p.a.) = 0.64 +
0.38 change in real M4 (per cent p.a.)
$R^2 = 0.28$
t statistic on regression coefficient = 2.95

The econometrics here are primitive, but three comments seem in order. The first is that naive monetarism works better than naive fiscalism over both the whole period and in each of the three sub-periods (see Figure 2, comparing the changes in real M4 and real domestic demand over the whole period). Naive fiscalism was, however, only slightly worse than naive monetarism in the first sub-period (the period of 'the Keynesian revolution'). The second is that in the final sub-period, when medium-term fiscal rules prevailed, the relationship between changes in the budget deficit and domestic demand disappeared. The results of the naive fiscalist equation in the 1981–2004 period are atrocious: see Figure 3, with its obvious absence of a relationship; the R^2 is virtually nothing, and the regression coefficient has the wrong sign and is insignificant. It is not going too far to say that – in these years – naive Keynesianism was invalid, while the standard prescription of its supporters ('fiscal reflation will boost employment') was bunk. The third is that the 364 were not entirely silly to believe in 1981 that a reduction in the budget deficit would be deflationary. Although the relationship between the changes in the cyclically adjusted budget deficit and domestic demand had been worse than that between changes in real M4 and domestic demand in the preceding fifteen years, the naive fiscalist hypothesis had not done all that badly in the second sub-period. Indeed, by the careful selection of years one period of twenty years (1954 to 1973 inclusive) could be found with quite a strong relationship between fiscal policy and demand outcomes (see Figure 4.) It was only in the final 25 years of the post-war period that – on the analysis here – a naive Keynesian view of national income determination became indefensible.

The extremely poor quality of the fiscal equation in the final sub-period raises the question 'Was its better performance in the two previous sub-periods really because fiscal policy *by itself* was quite powerful or was it rather because fiscal policy influenced money supply growth and monetary policy was the relevant, strong influence on demand?' To answer these questions, the author regressed the rate of real M4 growth on both the level and the change in the PSFD/GDP ratio over the whole 1949–2004 period, and each of the sub-periods, and was unable to find a relationship between the variables that met standard criteria of statistical significance. Much more analysis could be done, but the apparent conclusion cannot be denied. To the extent that fiscal policy was effective between 1949 and 1980, it did not work largely through monetary policy and had some independent effect on the economy. This may provide solace to those (presumably most of the 364) who claim that fiscal policy mattered in these years, even though fiscal policy plainly did not matter after 1980 and monetary policy has always mattered more.

In his celebrated attack on 'the new monetarism' in the July 1970 issue of *Lloyds Bank Review*, Kaldor scorned the role of monetary policy by claiming that changes in money supply growth could be 'explained' by fiscal policy. In his words, 'I am convinced that the short-run variations in the "money supply" – in other words, the variation relative to trend – are very largely explained by the variation in the public sector's borrowing requirement.'

He amplified the point in a footnote which read:

> In fact, a simple regression equation of the annual change
> of the money supply on the public sector borrowing
> requirement for the years 1954–68 shows that the money
> supply increased almost exactly £ for £ with every £1
> increase in the public sector deficit, with $t = 6.1$ and R^2

Figure 2 **Money growth and demand, 1949–2004**
%

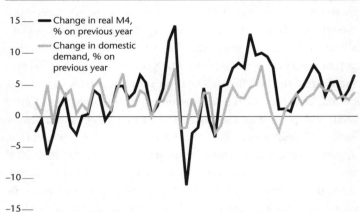

= 0.740, or, in fashionable language, 74 per cent of the
variation in the money supply is explained by the deficit of
the public sector alone.[27]

The results of the regression reported in Kaldor's footnote
are surprising, since the PSBR was not introduced as an official
statistic until 1963 and (unless he had access to internal Treasury
estimates, which is possible) no such regression could have been
carried out for earlier years. The author has tried to replicate
Kaldor's result by regressing the change in 'the money supply'
(i.e. the sum of notes and coin in circulation and clearing bank

---

27   Nicholas Kaldor, 'The new monetarism', *Lloyds Bank Review*, July 1970, pp. 1–17,
reprinted in Sir Alan Walters (ed.), *Money and Banking*, Harmondsworth: Pen-
guin, 1973, pp. 261–78. See, in particular, p. 277.

Figure 3   **Fiscal policy and demand, 1981–2004 ('the period of medium-term fiscal rules')**

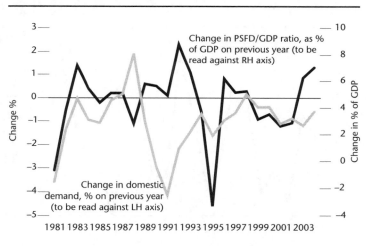

deposits) on the public sector financial deficit, for which (to repeat) data are available back to 1948. The equation was markedly worse than the one reported by Kaldor (with a regression coefficient of 0.48, an R^2 of 0.38 and a t statistic of 2.81), but it was not poor. It is indeed plausible that – in the 1950s and 1960s, when bank lending to the private sector was officially restricted for much of the time – a major influence on the growth of banks' balance sheets was the increase in their holdings of public sector debt. Fiscal and debt management policies *did* affect money supply growth, as most economists thought at the time (and despite the results mentioned two paragraphs above).

This does not mean, however – as Kaldor seems to have implied – that in all circumstances fiscal policy dominated

Figure 4   **Fiscal policy and demand, 1954–73 ('the heyday of the Keynesian revolution')**

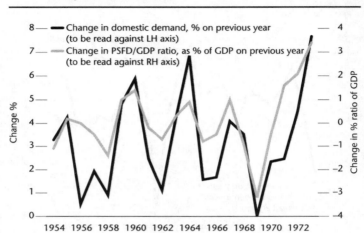

monetary policy and that monetary policy *by itself* was unimportant. In the 1980s and 1990s, after the removal of credit restrictions, bank lending to the private sector became by far the largest credit counterpart of M4 growth, and the change in money and the budget deficit were no longer correlated. But – as this Annex has shown – the influence of money on demand remained identifiable, whereas the influence of fiscal policy on demand vanished. In retrospect it is clear that Kaldor went too far in his statement about the link between the budget deficit and money growth.[28]

---

28   The breakdown of 'Kaldor's rule' was noted in J. H. B. Tew, 'Monetary policy', in F. T. Blackaby (ed.), *British Economic Policy 1960–74*, Cambridge: Cambridge University Press, 1978, ch. 5, pp. 218–303. See, particularly, pp. 277–8. Ironically, for those concerned that excessive money supply growth would lead to inflation, Kaldor's rule justified official action to constrain the budget deficit, as

He did at least recognise, however, that fiscal variables, and not monetary variables alone, needed to be cited as evidence in the debate. British Keynesians have later been much too ready to debunk monetary aggregates. The same standards of proof need to be applied to both monetary *and fiscal* variables.

incorporated in the Conservatives' medium-term financial strategy from 1980.

2 THE BUDGET OF 1981 WAS OVER THE TOP[1]
Stephen Nickell

Introduction

After the 1981 Budget, 364 university economists in Britain wrote to complain about the tightness of macroeconomic policy, prompted by the plans in the Budget to cut public sector borrowing by some £3.3 billion, mainly by increasing taxes. It is now a commonplace view that the 364 were wrong to complain because, shortly after publication of the letter, the growth rate of real domestic demand and GDP in the UK switched from negative to positive. As it happens this view is incorrect. As one of the 364, I would say that, wouldn't I? So in what follows I pursue this question by analysing the periods before and after the sending of the letter. I conclude that the 364 economists were perfectly correct to complain about the macroeconomic policy of the day back in 1981.

Why sign the letter?

I signed the letter because, at the time, I had long thought that monetary policy was too tight and that tightening fiscal policy in early 1981 was a mistake. While it was true that the letter was not everything I might have wished for, it was the only show in town,

---

1   I am grateful to Chris Shadforth for his help in the preparation of this paper.

and I felt that I should stand up and be counted. In particular, I had always believed that the world was best understood in a NAIRU[2] framework, and indeed at the time I was busy trying to estimate the path of equilibrium unemployment in Britain (see Nickell, 1982). So it is no surprise that I did not find the implicit theoretical analysis underlying points a) and d) in the letter entirely to my taste. I approved wholeheartedly, however, of the main points b) and c), and still do.[3] So how might they be justified in the light of the fact, already noted, that output growth in Britain turned positive shortly after the letter appeared? Surely, it is typically argued, all this talk of deepening depression must be so much hot air in the light of this fact. Fortunately for me, this argument is just wrong. For the depression to deepen or the output gap to become more negative, output growth does not have to be negative, it merely has to be below trend. So the 364 cannot simply be dismissed out of hand by pointing to the time series of GDP growth. More analysis is required.

What happened before the Budget of 1981?

When the Thatcher government took office in the spring of 1979, annual inflation (GDP deflator) was close to 11 per cent and had fallen steadily since peaking at over 25 per cent in 1975 after the disaster of the first oil shock. This fall in inflation had been

---

2   'Non-accelerating inflation rate of unemployment'. Broadly this means the rate below which unemployment cannot fall without inflation rising.

3   The letter is reproduced in the Appendix but, in summary, (a) stated that there was no basis or evidence in economic theory that government policies would permanently reduce inflation; (b) stated that the present policies would deepen the depression; (c) stated that there were alternative policies; and (d) stated that the time had come to reject monetarist policies and pursue alternatives.

engineered essentially by trying to use an incomes policy to lower the equilibrium rate of unemployment with actual unemployment fairly stable. In the years leading up to 1979, unemployment had been around 6 per cent using the OECD measure and somewhat lower using the Department of Employment (DE) measure (see Layard et al., 1991: Table A3). During this period and for many years before, wages tended to respond rapidly to changes in retail price index (RPI) inflation unless obstructed by incomes policy; inflation expectations were not stable (as far as we know); and there was no belief in the labour market that government macroeconomic policy would respond aggressively to inflationary shocks.

Aside from scrapping the incomes policy, the change of government had little impact on these features of the labour market. The rapid response of wages to changes in RPI inflation, now completely unconstrained by incomes policy, was perfectly exemplified by the year following the first Budget of the new administration in June 1979. The main feature of this Budget was the switch from income taxes to VAT. This plus the rise in oil prices raised RPI inflation by over five percentage points between the second and third quarters of 1979, so that after a wage–price spiral (see Figure 5), by the second quarter of 1980, RPI inflation was 21.5 per cent, wage inflation was 21.3 per cent and the GDP deflator was rising at 22.3 per cent. Wage inflation continued to rise, reaching 22.4 per cent in the third quarter, by which time the rise in VAT had dropped out of the RPI and things started to subside.[4] Monetary policy responded aggressively to this infla-

---

4   While the report of the Clegg Commission on Public Sector Pay was important for those working in the public sector, its consequences for overall wage inflation were not large. Were Figure 5 to be based on private sector wage inflation, it

Figure 5   **Inflation, 1978–82**
Percentage change on a year ago

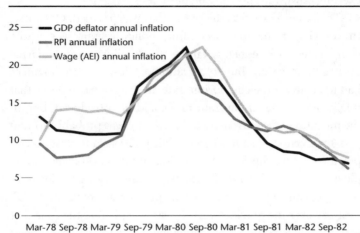

tionary shock with the interest rate used for monetary policy purposes reaching 17 per cent in November 1979, having been at 12 per cent when Mrs Thatcher took office.

So now the basic problem was to get inflation back down again, preferably to some reasonable level, in a world where, as we have seen, governments had little anti-inflation credibility. There is no option in this situation but to use a tight macroeconomic policy to raise unemployment well above the equilibrium rate and then wait for inflation to subside, before gradually loosening policy. The whole process is tricky, all the more so because if some of the unemployed become detached from the labour market after

would look very similar. The public sector was not big enough to have a dramatic impact.

being unemployed for a long time, they are no longer so useful at exerting downward pressure on pay rises.

This, in essence, was the policy that was pursued. Of course, the details of the macroeconomic policy regime were quite complicated with monetary targets, the Medium Term Financial Strategy and so on. But to get inflation down, unemployment had to go above the equilibrium rate. In due course, policies that might reduce the equilibrium rate could be introduced, but, in the meantime, the current equilibrium rate was probably around 7 to 8 per cent and so macroeconomic policy had to push unemployment above this level. By the time of the 1981 Budget, unemployment was rising rapidly thanks to the very tight monetary policy, having increased by some 4.2 percentage points on the DE measure over the previous year. It was also plain at the time that with unchanged policies, unemployment was going to rise a good bit farther, UK relative unit labour costs having risen by 44 per cent since 1978 thanks to North Sea oil and high interest rates.

So at the time of the 1981 Budget, the current and prospective path of unemployment was easily going to be high enough to bring down inflation to normal levels in a reasonable time. Indeed, I would have argued that monetary policy could have been eased somewhat without endangering the steady downward path of inflation. So what happened in the 1981 Budget and beyond?

What happened after the Budget of 1981?

As we have seen, planned fiscal policy was tightened significantly in the 1981 Budget and, at the same time, interest rates were cut from 14 per cent to 12 per cent. They were, however, raised back to 14 per cent on 15 September and to 15 per cent on 12 October, so

Figure 6   **Unemployment and inflation, 1976–90**
Percentage change on a year ago and unemployment rate

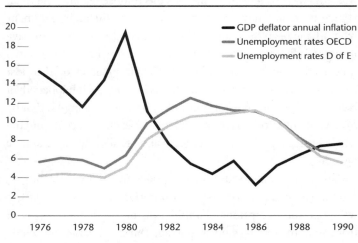

the monetary easing was temporary. In the complaint of the 364 economists, it was argued that the depression would deepen. So what happened? Despite positive output growth, unemployment continued to rise (see Figure 6). Unemployment peaked on the OECD measure at 12.5 per cent in 1983 but did not fall below 11 per cent until 1987. On the DE measure, unemployment continued to rise, year on year, until it peaked at 11.2 per cent in 1986. Under the not unreasonable assumption that rising unemployment means that growth is below trend (there being no reason to believe equilibrium unemployment was rising much between 1982 and 1986), the depression deepened until somewhere between 1983 and 1986, exactly as the 364 said it would. Even though unemployment has to be above the equilibrium rate to get inflation down, this strikes me as overkill. By the time of the 1981 Budget, monetary policy was already too tight. It could have been loosened and the fiscal stance need not have been tightened and still unemployment would have been far enough above the equilibrium rate to have brought inflation down. Maybe it would not have come down quite so fast, but with the fall in oil prices in 1986, it would almost certainly have been at reasonable levels by 1987. As it happened, of course, by 1987 macroeconomic policy became so gung-ho that by 1990 GDP inflation was back at its 1982 level (7.6 per cent) and the whole business had to be repeated in an only slightly less dramatic fashion.

So is there any excuse for the policy overkill which the 364 economists complained about so bitterly? One possible excuse was that the exceptionally rapid rate of productivity growth from 1982 to 1986 was not expected. During this period, whole economy productivity growth was close to 3 per cent. This was not just a cyclical recovery and was unusually high by recent historical standards (see Nickell et al., 1992, for some explanations). So over this period, trend growth rates would have been especially high, particularly relative to the 1970s. This would make it more likely that macroeconomic policy would be set in such a way as to generate output growth at a rate lower than would be desirable. And this is exactly what happened.

Conclusions

The main complaint of the 364 economists in their 1981 letter was that macroeconomic policy was unnecessarily tight and that it would deepen the depression. By ensuring that subsequent output growth was below trend for a number of years, it did indeed deepen the depression just as predicted. Furthermore, it was unnecessarily tight in the sense that a somewhat looser policy would still have raised unemployment far enough above its equilibrium level to bring inflation down over a reasonable period. So in their key comments on the facts of the case, the 364 economists turned out to be completely correct.

References

Layard, R., S. Nickell and R. Jackman (1991), *Unemployment, Macroeconomic Performance and the Labour Market*, Oxford: Oxford University Press.

Nickell, S. J. (1982), 'The determinants of equilibrium unemployment in Britain', *Economic Journal*, 92: 555–75, September.

Nickell, S., S. Wadhwani and M. Wall (1992), 'Productivity growth in UK companies, 1975–1986', *European Economic Review*, 36: 1055–91.

3   CAN 364 ECONOMISTS BE WRONG?
Geoffrey E. Wood

Prologue: 364 economists reconsidered

I cannot remember whether it was my idea to write a commentary in *Economic Affairs* when the letter from the 364 economists appeared in *The Times* or whether it was Arthur Seldon's idea. Arthur Seldon was the editor of *Economic Affairs* at the time. It is, indeed, a long time since I looked at or even thought about the article. When Philip Booth asked me to write a chapter for a monograph on the 25th anniversary of the famous letter, I therefore wondered whether or not I would feel grateful to Arthur Seldon for publishing my original article all those years ago.

Reading the famous letter and my commentary on it again did lead to some feelings of regret; but these were over my comments on the policies of the then government, which the letter's signatories were condemning, and most certainly not over my comments on the letter itself.

In fact I could only marvel at what strikes me now with even more force than it did then – how could the signatories misrepresent so much published and therefore publicly available work, and ignore so many facts? My article of 25 years ago needs neither apology nor emendation so far as its comments on the letter go. Indeed, I would now put my criticism more strongly than I did 25 years ago.

Over the years since the publication of my article I have, thanks to the prompting and collaboration of my colleague the distinguished economic historian Forrest Capie, worked increasingly on monetary history. This has primarily been on that of the UK, although from time to time on that of other countries also. We have looked at data from the past 300 years. Never for any time, apart from the extraordinary circumstances of total war, or for any country, have we found a study or produced a finding that showed inflation to result from anything other than excess monetary ease. Never have we found an example of inflation being reduced by any means other than ending that monetary ease. Yet the 364 signatories attacked policies of which the fundamental premise was the link between money and inflation. When I wrote my article I marvelled at the evidence the 364 had ignored. My marvel now is the greater, as my knowledge of just how much they ignored has grown.

Why did so many ignore so much? Curiously, in the very same issue of *Economic Affairs* as originally contained my article, there was an article by Lionel Robbins which hinted at the answer. Robbins pointed out that the IEA had '... made a major contribution to the rehabilitation of the market as an institution'. The IEA had helped show the dangers of '... an economic structure which rests excessively on collectivist decisions'. In showing that, the IEA was fighting against the intellectual fashion in Britain. If one subscribes to that fashion and is of a collectivist mind, so that one wants the state to have a large part in managing the details of economic life, then the apparatus of controls, incomes policies and direction of labour and resources seems natural and desirable. It would be straying too far in this short note to enter into speculation as to just why that cast of mind was so fashionable in Britain in the years after World War II until the early 1980s (and indeed still is); those interested in pursuing the matter will find a most promising introduction to it in a recent publication by Tim Congdon (2004).

I must end with an apology. In my article I criticised, quite harshly, the then government of the day. My complaint was that while they had promised excellent policies their execution of them had been distinctly defective. In making that criticism I paid too little heed to the difficulties of public expenditure control, and to the effects that major changes in the financial system had produced in the short-term relationship between inflation and various monetary aggregates. With hindsight it is clear to me that the government that was in office from 1979 to 1983 initiated a set of policies and, more importantly, an approach to policy-making from which the British economy is still benefiting today.

Can 364 economists be wrong?[1]

In March 1981, 364 academic economists published a short memorandum highly critical of government policy. The weight of such opinion seems impressive. It is hard to believe there can not be something wrong with policies subject to such an attack. And there is indeed a lot wrong. But the 364 signatories totally misunderstood what it is.

They criticised what the government said it was going to do – and the government's intentions are admirable. But the signatories have failed to see that the government has carried out almost

---

1   This is the text of Geoffrey Wood's article of the same title in *Economic Affairs*, July 1981.

none of its intentions. There has indeed been a failure, but of execution, not of intention.

The signatories' criticism

What did the signatories put their name to? Their statement was in four sections:

(a) There is no basis in economic theory or supporting evidence for the Government's belief that, by deflating demand, they will bring inflation permanently under control and thereby induce an automatic recovery in output and employment.

That proposition totally misrepresents the theory and evidence that underline the government's intentions. Temporarily 'deflating demand' will not permanently bring inflation under control. No economic model purports to show that. What a substantial body of evidence *does* show is that the trend of money growth determines the trend of inflation; the control of the rate of growth of money is therefore necessary to control the rate of growth of prices. What has that got to do with 'deflating demand'? There may temporarily be a connection, as money growth is reduced from an excessive rate to one consistent with a tolerable inflation rate, but that 'deflation' will be, *at worst*, short lived.

Since the core of the government's intentions is the reduction of inflation, it is worth developing that argument. First, it is quite beside the point to argue, as some ill-informed critics of monetarism do, that control of money will not give perfect control of prices. Monetarists recognise this perfectly well. Many factors apart from money growth can affect the general level of prices. A harvest failure or an increase in the price of oil are both good examples. But such factors affect the price level through changes in relative prices; unless they are *continual*, they will not affect the rate of inflation.

Further, and much more important, government cannot do anything about them. In contrast, if government controls the money supply it is controlling the inflation-causing factor that is within its influence. That is what monetarists ask government to do, not to work miracles and remove all adverse shocks from the world. There is certainly no evidence that the growth of money at a low and steady rate rather than a high and steady rate affects aggregate demand. Once inflation has been brought down, keeping it down will not 'deflate demand'.

Moreover, it is not clear that the process of bringing down the rate of growth in the money supply must deflate demand. There is a lot of analytical work (most notably Lucas, 1972) which indicates that only *unanticipated* changes in the rate of growth of money affect *demand*, and that *anticipated* changes affect only prices. Evidence to support this proposition is not easy to develop, in part because of the difficulty in distinguishing between anticipated and unanticipated changes. But evidence is certainly starting to accumulate that if monetary changes are anticipated, their real effect is much diminished (see Barro and Rush, 1980). Hence, far from the Thatcher government seeking to 'deflate demand', its policy of announcing money growth in advance was designed to minimise the effects on demand of the anti-inflation policy.

The price of mastering inflation

Probably some deflation, although modest, is an inevitable part of reducing inflation. Is this price worth paying? The answer must be an unequivocal yes – for the factors that produce a fall in demand following a monetary squeeze also contribute to making inflation very damaging to the economy.

Relative prices are not equally flexible. Some respond instantly to a change in the balance of supply and demand; others are slow. Hence when there is a monetary squeeze price increases do not all slow down immediately. In consequence, as some goods (and factors of production) become temporarily more expensive, demand for them drops. A recession from this cause is probably an inevitable consequence of reducing inflation.

This very same price stickiness makes inflation expensive to tolerate. As inflation accelerates, uncertainty about prices intensifies, and quite understandably, because the variability of inflation seems to increase with the rate. (If the annual rate of inflation is 10 per cent, it will vary from around, say, 8 per cent to 12 per cent, and if at 20 per cent from, say, 16 per cent to 24 per cent.) In consequence resources are misallocated, both because of this uncertainty and because of the temporary distortion of relative prices. Theories or explanations that minimise or ignore the cost of inflation omit an important feature of the world. It is worth reducing inflation to low single figures – and preferably to zero. There are costs – but the costs of not reducing inflation are higher.

What of the 'automatic recovery in output and employment' that the 364 claim is supposed to be coming? What is really at issue here is whether an economy that has sustained a severe shock, causing a major deficiency of demand, can recover without a stimulus. In some theories, excess supply can persist for ever by assuming permanent price stickiness. (It is equally possible to envisage conditions where excess supply never appears at all.) Now, explanations with permanent excess supply depend on price rigidities; and what of course matters is not that such theories can be constructed but whether or not they are good approximations to reality.

Prices are sticky, not rigid

Prices undoubtedly are sticky and can thereby produce excess supply for some time. But sticky is not the same as rigid. History indicates that long-lasting depressions – notably the Great Depression of 1929–32 – have been the result of a series of deflationary shocks impinging on the economy as a consequence of mistakes in policy. Such depressions are therefore *not* evidence of a tendency of economies to stay in recession for ever. Rather they show the damage that can be done by incompetent policy. That it took such incompetence to cause long-lasting depressions does not prove that they are impossible without failure in policy. It is hard to prove a negative. But it does show that the possibility of such recessions has yet to be demonstrated in practice.

That is why, although the removal of inflation from the system will not 'induce' a recovery in output, it will certainly not prevent it either.

Eroding the industrial base

The second part of the statement was that:

(b) Present policies will deepen the depression, erode the

industrial base of our economy, and threaten its social and political stability.

The latter part of this assertion is not an economic issue, although it is rather like a petulant child threatening to do terrible things if he does not get what he wants. Will the industrial base of the economy be 'eroded'? What if it is? Do economies have to be industrialised to be prosperous? None of the signatories can believe that; if they do, they should consider the example of Switzerland, which demonstrates that supplying services can make a society at least as prosperous as can supplying goods. Will the 'erosion' be permanent? Suppose some industries do close down in consequence of a monetary squeeze; why should they not recover? There is undoubtedly the task of regaining lost market shares; but that would be a serious problem only if the industries were out of the market for a long time. If the industries were capable of competing in the longer term, a temporary squeeze at home would affect profits, but be unlikely to produce closure. Even if it did, once the firm had closed down and the fixed costs were written off, it could be revived (see Tullock, 1981). The idea that a basically sound industry can be 'eroded' by a temporary squeeze reveals a fundamental failure to understand how markets and prices work.

What are 'the alternatives'?

The third part of the 364's statement hinted, cryptically, at 'alternative policies'.

To say that there are alternatives is true but vacuous. It is always possible to attempt to swim from London to New York.

What is rather more interesting is whether the swimmer will arrive. Will the alternatives work? The final part of the statement was:

> The time has come to reject monetarist policies and consider urgently which alternative offers the best hope of sustained economic recovery.

Monetarist principles are consistent with a very large body of evidence. It is, indeed, a mistake to describe what the Thatcher government is doing as an 'experiment in the UK'. We have seen the effects of monetary policy in the UK often enough. What is unfortunate is that these effects have usually been in one direction – towards faster inflation. The most notable example is the monetary and fiscal promiscuity that occurred during the Heath–Barber years. These excesses, it should be observed, did not produce a permanently higher level of *output*. All they gave, after a *temporary* fillip to demand, was a higher rate of *inflation*. The 364 imply that monetarist policies are not supported by evidence. It is one of the best-established propositions of economics that faster money growth leads to faster inflation, and slower money growth to slower inflation.

That is not to say that present policies have been perfect.

The government's words ...

The government's *words* have been monetarist. The clearest statement is in the 'Red Book' which accompanied the 1980/81 Budget: 'To reduce inflation it [i.e. the Government] will progressively reduce the rate of growth of the money stock ...'

That expresses the central tenet of monetarism – and, as

argued above, it is consistent with a good deal of evidence, including UK data ('Background to the Government's economic strategy', Treasury memorandum prepared for the Select Committee on the Treasury and Civil Service).

The government has also committed itself to doing other things — it has been *market-oriented*, as well as monetarist. The public sector has to be slimmed, and made more efficient. Obstacles to the growth of the private sector are to be removed. Subsidies to inefficient firms are to be abolished. Taxes are to be cut. So is public sector borrowing.

None of this is specifically 'monetarist' in a narrow sense. Nonetheless, most monetarists would support these policies – in part because underlying monetarism is a scepticism about the ability of government to 'manage' the economy in detail. Further, cutting the PSBR, while not essential for monetary control, does undoubtedly facilitate such control, given the methods of controlling monetary growth in the UK.

The whole package of statements, then, although not purely monetarist, is consistent with monetarist sympathies and proclivities. Are the results claimed for the package supported by theory and evidence?

These issues were examined by Roy Batchelor in the preceding issue of this *Journal* ('Thatcherism could succeed', *JEA*, vol. 1, no. 3). So long as markets are used to guide resource allocation, signals of relative scarcities are provided by prices. This signalling system is certainly not perfect; there is an extensive literature dealing with causes of 'market failure'. But acknowledgment of its imperfections does not necessarily mean that the system must be abandoned. Available alternatives must be evaluated.

Much work, originating in Professor R. H. Coase's 'The

problem of social cost' (*Journal of Law and Economics*, 1960), has evaluated the alternative to the price system for the guidance of resource allocation. The conclusion of this work is unambiguous. *The available alternatives are much worse than reliance on the price system.*

Allowing capital and goods markets to work freely, thereby speeding the transfer of resources from sectors of the economy not exposed to market pressures to sectors which are (that is, basically from public to private sector), is what the government should do to facilitate economic growth and prosperity. This is the best policy, not because the market is perfect, but because the market is less imperfect than the alternatives. The more successful the government is in freeing resources for the market sector, the more efficient, and the more prosperous, the economy will be.

... have belied its deeds

The government's deeds have, unfortunately, not accorded with their principles. The critique, indeed, could have united all the 364 – and many other economists. The criticism could be made on two planes. First, there is the very general one that to announce a set of policies and then not carry them out creates unnecessary uncertainty. No serious economist would claim that the creation of uncertainty is a task of government.

Second, there are specific criticisms. The government set a monetary target in terms of £M3.[2] This target was grossly

---

2   M1 = notes and coins in circulation with the public, plus UK private sector sterling sight deposits (encashable on demand). £M3 = M1 plus UK private sector sterling time deposits (not encashable on demand), plus public sector sterling deposits. Source: *Bank of England Quarterly Bulletin*.

exceeded. It was argued in the *Bank of England Quarterly Bulletin* (March 1981) that this was an inappropriate variable, and that monetary policy last year really was as tight as intended. Evidence advanced for this is the behaviour of M1, and in some quarters the behaviour of the exchange rate and interest rates.

It is possible to show, on both analytical and empirical grounds, that the last two are poor indicators of what monetary policy is going to do to inflation. The basic reason is straightforward; these variables are affected by non-monetary policy. The evidence against M1 is purely empirical. In the past, £M3 has been a better indicator of future inflation than has M1. This relationship may not last for ever: indeed, it may no longer be true. But in the light of currently available evidence, the government was correct to choose £M3 as their monetary target, and it therefore follows that last year's overshoot was a gross failure of policy.

That criticism is contentious and, as it is based purely on empirical support, may turn out to be invalid. Certain other criticisms of the government's budgetary policy are solidly rooted in a body of widely accepted economic analysis. The PSBR overshot its target by a very substantial margin. The excuse advanced is that the recession boosted 'uncontrollable' items such as the cost of unemployment benefit. That just does not fit the facts. A good part of the overshoot is clearly due to the government's failure to control discretionary elements of its own spending. This control may be hard to exercise, but the government was elected on a platform that embodied a commitment to exercise such control. Did the government promise to deliver something it knew it could not?

The damage done by this overshoot was compounded by the government's response to it. In an effort to gain control of the

PSBR in the absence of spending control, taxes were raised. Being unwilling to reverse their original tax decisions, the government made ill-judged changes in indirect taxes, in natural insurance contributions, and in the amount of income at which income tax becomes payable. The first exacerbated inflationary expectations at a time when it was desirable to reduce them. The second increased the costs of employing labour at a time when unemployment was in any event rising because of other factors. The third made the 'poverty trap' wider and deeper, reducing the incentive to work and indeed thereby increasing the government's budgetary problems.

Thus, far from transferring resources to the market sector, the government squeezed it by policies that augmented the harm such a squeeze was likely to do. There is ample scope for criticism of the government. It is a pity the 364 did not direct their fire better.

What are the alternatives?

One set of alternatives is clear. The government should do what it said it intended. That would not take us to nirvana; but it would take us in the direction we wish to go. The 364 did not say what alternative policies they had in mind. Their difficulties in producing such proposals are substantial.

Do they wish a fiscal stimulus to be applied? If so, they will have to show precisely the mistakes in the analytical and empirical literature (originated by Professor Robert Mundell when working at the IMF) which demonstrates that fiscal policy is impotent to affect aggregate demand when the exchange rate is floating. They may wish to argue that it is correct – but only in equilibrium, in the long run, and that there are transitional effects. That is true, but the evidence is that, in this case, we get close to the long run rather quickly, certainly within a year.

Do they want a monetary stimulus? If so, the issue of inflation becomes pressing. Do they wish to rely on prices and incomes policies? So far, as is widely acknowledged, they have failed. They may have deferred inflation, but they have always broken down, and then inflation has caught us up again. It will not do to say we should have a permanent policy. Prices and incomes policies have always been crumbling before they have been removed. We have to be shown a policy that will not crumble. All serious economists would be willing to consider such a proposal – if only to reduce the transitional output costs of reducing inflation. But is it not reasonable, in view of the failure of such policies in the past, to wait to see the proposal before deciding to implement it?

There may be workable alternatives to what the government said it would do, but we have yet to see them.

Conclusions

364 economists *can* be wrong. Indeed, the 364 signatories were doubly wrong. They criticised the principles of government policy – which are better founded than others set. They failed to criticise the implementation of policy – which has been extraordinarily bad. If the petition has any effect on policy it must be hoped the effect is to jolt the government back to doing what it intended – rather than being buffeted by the pleas and obstructions of special interests, with a high, avoidable cost being paid to the obstructers by the rest of the community.

References

Barro, R. J. and M. Rush (1980), 'Unanticipated money and economic activity', in Stanley Fischer (ed.), *Rational Expectations and Economic Policy*, Chicago, IL: University of Chicago Press.

Congdon, T. (2004), 'Monetarism: a rejoinder', *World Economics*, 5(2): 171–97.

Lucas, R. E. (1972), 'Expectations and the neutrality of money', *Journal of Economic Theory*, 4

Tullock, G. (1981) 'How to denationalise steel – an economist's dream', *Economic Affairs*, 1(2).

4 THE 364 WERE CORRECT
Maurice Peston

Three questions

In assessing the wisdom of the letter signed by 364 economists in 1981, we need to examine economic performance in the last quarter of a century. In turn economic performance needs to be considered in the context of other economic developments. Thus, we need to consider three questions:

- what has changed in macroeconomic policy?;
- what has changed in the macro economy?; and
- how, if at all, have the two been related?

In addition, serious economists cannot avoid asking whether economic theory has played a part in any of this.

On the policy side we may note the following:

- Low inflation has replaced full employment as the primary policy target.
- Incomes policy has virtually disappeared, although a recent statement by the Chancellor of the Exchequer on public sector pay being limited to the rise in the consumer price index (which is typically lower than retail price index inflation) suggests that incomes policy is not yet dead.

- We now have explicit financial targets for the public sector coupled, presumably, with a willingness to accept job losses if spending exceeds targets. More generally, fiscal fine tuning has been abandoned, and fiscal rules are set for the medium term, involving, somewhat controversially, averaging out over the cycle.
- Monetary policy has been given a statutory basis and has been entrusted to an independent body, namely the Monetary Policy Committee of the Bank of England. In practice this has involved a great deal of interest rate fine tuning on their part,
- Trade union powers have been drastically reduced by legislative action.
- Starting from when Geoffrey Howe was Chancellor of the Exchequer, the economy has been made more open, both with respect to trade in goods and services, and capital movements. Of course, a great deal of protection and restrictive practices remain.
- Microeconomic policies have been proposed, especially as a means of employment creation and reduction of unemployment. Whether we are talking about better education and training, diminished employee protection, greater labour mobility and the acceptance that jobs are no longer for life, there is nothing new to consider. What is remarkable is the apparent willingness of politicians in this country to adopt such measures. In his 1984 Mais Lecture, Chancellor of the Exchequer Nigel Lawson did, in fact, state that microeconomic measures should be the policy instrument that was used to achieve employment objectives and that macroeconomic policy should be used to control

inflation (see the chapter by Derek Scott in this volume). I doubt, however, whether he would have envisaged such microeconomic activism in the pursuit of employment objectives. (It is also worth recalling Keynes's observation that if we established full employment, the market economy would then work in the way set out in the microeconomics of his day. This is far from saying that a good microenvironment could be a substitute for macro policy.)

On the factual side relevant developments are these:

- The inflation rate has fallen, especially compared with the high levels of the 1970s. Prices, however, have risen throughout the period.
- Unemployment has risen, and at no time since 1980 has there been full employment.
- GDP growth has remained stubbornly at its long-term average of 2.5 per cent p.a. A failure to deal rapidly and properly with the inevitable real-income loss necessitated by the oil price rise took the economy off track in the 1970s, but that seems to have had no lasting effect.
- Since the mid-1990s (but not before) GDP growth and the inflation rate have been remarkably stable.
- Trade union membership has declined significantly, especially in the private sector, as have days lost from strikes.
- The current account of the balance of payments has been in deficit since 1984, the worst year being 1989, but with one exception (in the Lamont years) there has been nothing resembling an external crisis.
- The overall fiscal position has also stayed under control, with

the deficit generally being within the target range. There is controversy as to whether the financing requirement this year really has moved away from the target, and whether drastic fiscal intervention is required. But that is certainly not clear cut. More interesting is that, given the fuss being made by supposedly expert commentators, gilts continue to be sold without too much, if any, difficulty at low nominal and real yields.

Relating the outcomes to the policies, it is not surprising that setting an inflation target has led to lower price rises and a more stable rate of price increases. Inflation has not been abolished, although there is a tendency in some places to interpret what has happened as if that were the case.

It is also not surprising that abandoning full employment as the main macroeconomic objective has led to persistent unemployment. Indeed, if it is measured correctly, we are well away from what used to be thought desirable both as regards economic efficiency as well as equity.

Thus, economists may be reassured that the outcomes have been exactly what was predicted by the 364 economists all those years ago. What theory said would happen did happen. This is especially the case if the weakening of the powers of the trade unions is brought into the picture. Clearly, that made for an easier policy environment in that internally generated cost-push factors have been moderated. Speaking for myself alone, I did not foresee the introduction of the relevant legislation and the change in the policy environment. To be set against that, it is not at all clear that the unemployment costs of inflation reduction and control have been moderated.

What is harder to explain is the external side. Has the underlying cause of the persistent balance of payments deficit been too low a level of domestic net saving, leading to higher interest and exchange rates? Or has inflation targeting led to higher interest rates which, coupled with growing confidence on the part of foreign investors, generated an excessive capital inflow? What of the argument that GDP has been too high relative to capacity, implying either a fall in the rate of exchange (which gets in the way of anti-inflation policy) or a persistent current account deficit?

Although I have a view on all that, it would be inappropriate to expound it at length now. What I can say is that the economic analysis of all these matters has not changed much over the last quarter of a century, which is helpful in informing our understanding of whether the 364 economists were correct.

Conclusion

Economics journals continue to be full of weird and wonderful theories, which are for the most part rehashes of earlier weird and wonderful theories. What has changed is that it is now absolutely necessary to formulate everything in high-powered mathematical terms. I know I should be accused of churlishness if I were to add that this is intended largely to disguise the essential triviality of what is set forth. Occasionally, something of intellectual interest emerges, and there is even the odd article that throws light on the real world. Econometrics too gets more and more sophisticated, but rarely is anything of value discovered (I must say this is quite different from what I expected when I first went to work for Oscar Morgenstern 50 years ago).

But, in a direct practical sense, except possibly within the ECB, monetarism, and especially an emphasis on the money supply, is dead. Of greater interest is that while policy objectives change, the way we do economics remains recognisably Keynesian. No so-called micro-foundation is a substitute for the macro-models that we actually concentrate on. More to the point, when the MPC, for example, sets out its analysis of any of its policy interventions, it does so in terms which Bill Phillips[1] would have recognised 40 years ago, and Keynes himself would have had no difficulty with 20 years earlier.

1   Originator of the 'Phillips curve'.

5   THE LETTER FROM THE 364
ECONOMISTS – A DANGEROUS AND
DISHONEST GAME
Patrick Minford

Introduction

When the 364 economists wrote to *The Times* in 1981, I responded
with an article that was published in that paper on 7 April 1981.
My contribution to this IEA volume is simply to reproduce that
article. Nothing has changed that has led me to revise my view
that the 364 were playing a dangerous and dishonest game. I
regarded it as a dangerous and dishonest game, rather than
simply misguided, for two reasons. It was dangerous because
ministers, who are untrained in economics, rely on hard-headed
professionals to help them resist the siren voices that would have
them make a U-turn when the pursuit of the correct policies leads
to temporary discomfort. It was dishonest because the weight of
evidence that suggested the 364 were wrong was before their very
eyes: indeed, much of the evidence was produced by economists
who would have called themselves 'Keynesian'.

A dangerous and dishonest game

The 364 'Keynesians' who signed last week's statement attacking
the government's handling of the economy have forgotten some
salient facts, which would not have escaped their master. The
public sector accounts in 1932, the trough of the Great Depression,

appear to have been in significant financial surplus when adjusted for the economic cycle (i.e. after deducting the effects of the cycle on revenue and social expenditures). The money supply had grown at less than 1 per cent a year and prices had fallen by more than 2 per cent a year over the previous five years. So Keynes could rightly observe that the actual deficit could be increased with no threat to (indeed restoration of) price stability.

Today the public sector still has a massive borrowing requirement when adjusted for the cycle: in the fiscal year 1979/80 about 5 per cent of gross domestic product and in 1980/81 about 4 per cent. This has been sustaining high inflation. But the budget for 1981/82, if plans are fully carried out, will cut this percentage to about 1 per cent of GDP and lay the basis for permanently lower inflation, even eventual price stability.

While one can write pages of algebra and estimate scores of statistical relationships, the essentials of the inflationary process are simple. It starts when government, unwilling to cover its expenditure by overt taxation, borrows from the public.

As interest rates rise, in order to induce the public to lend, political pressures develop to hold them down. Lending to the government from the public slows down and the central bank has to lend the difference, which, of course, it does by increasing the supply of money.

During the early stages output usually rises, as extra monetary demand is met by producers whose expectations of inflation have not yet altered and who therefore think that rising prices offer them higher real returns. Expected inflation will soon increase, however, as information both about the policies and actually rising prices becomes widely known. This causes prices to rise faster and output to fall back.

At some point the increase in the rate of growth of money supply and so of monetary demand is entirely accounted for by an equal increase in inflation, and output has dropped right back to where it would have been.

This description is widely accepted by serious students of macroeconomics. True, there have been – and persist – differences of view, in particular about time lags and the interaction of fiscal and monetary influences. These differences ironically have been as great or even greater within the ranks of 'monetarists' than between them and 'Keynesians'. And the economists who have developed this general line of thinking include as many Keynesians as monetarists. Indeed, the mechanism is named after a Keynesian, A. W. Phillips, who taught at the London School of Economics in the 1950s.

Yet part (a) of the statement by the 364, on which the other parts are essentially based, explicitly rejects this mechanism in stating that 'deflating demand' will not 'bring inflation permanently under control' and thereby induce 'an automatic recovery in output and employment'. For, of course, that is precisely what the same mechanism asserts when the process of deficit and money creation is put into reverse, as the present government is doing.

Charity dictates that we interpret this rejection by 364 economists as an unintentional lapse; otherwise it would make nonsense of their professional work.

To carry out this reversal of the inflationary process, to break the inflation psychology, political courage and determination of a high order are necessary because of the short-term pressures that are generated – the strong vested interests on the expenditure side, the unpopularity of higher taxes, the temporary misery of the initial recession. At a certain point in the process the siren voices murmuring easy options can become irresistible; the minds of ministers, untrained in economics, can hardly be blamed for being easily seduced. But hard-headed professionals require our most severe censure if they back such nonsense.

One such suggestion is that instead of reducing inflation we should stabilise it at its existing level and 'live with it'. Yet recent studies have come up with very large costs for this option (e.g. Feldstein in 1979 for the USA, G. W. Hilliard and myself in 1978 for the United Kingdom), costs that appear to be far higher than any transitional loss of output that could be involved in eliminating inflation.

The more popular easy options are reflation to increase output, with incomes policy to prevent inflation, a view usually backed by the glib assertion that the economy suffers from widespread 'market failure'. This is the route both of some clever general equilibrium theorists and of others who are utterly ignorant of modern macroeconomics. But a convincing theoretical account of an economy that would respond as hoped to these policies has yet to be constructed.

The evidence is brutal. Incomes policies have broken down repeatedly since 1960, leaving no trace on the inflation rate. Reflation has been followed by inflation and output has continued to rise slowly, with the massive extra demand (e.g. real disposal incomes rose by more than 7 per cent per annum from 1977 to 1979) going into imports.

The effects of counter-inflationary policies have been superimposed on the adjustment to North Sea oil and a world recession of broadly the severity of that which took place in 1974/75. The strains on particular companies and industries in the international sector have been intense. But there is no evidence that those with sound long-term prospects are going to the wall. Instead, we have seen rationalisation, a reduction in over-manning and a sharp reduction in wage settlements. Indeed, the stock market is now increasing the capitalisation of even the hardest-hit sectors.

In the short run, this process worsens unemployment. But, in the long run, unemployment by general agreement can only be eliminated by this and other improvements in competitiveness. Bitter experience has confirmed what monetary theory predicts – that devaluation and incomes policies are incapable of raising competitiveness for more than a brief period. It is likely, however, that union power, high labour taxes and social security benefits and a heavily controlled housing market help to create serious unemployment and lower competitiveness.

Economic analysis can help to identify solutions. But the economist who downs tools to sign petitions for apparently political ends is playing a dangerous and dishonest game, even with 363 others.

6 364 ECONOMISTS AND ECONOMICS WITHOUT PRICES
Philip Booth

A personal note

When the 1981 Budget was presented to the House of Commons by Geoffrey Howe I was in the lower sixth at school. I was in my fourth year of studying economics, having been fortunate to attend a comprehensive school that taught the subject from age thirteen.[1] On leaving school I pursued economics at undergraduate level for a further three years from 1982 to 1985. I am contributing a chapter to this monograph not because I have any more to add to the macroeconomic debate than has already been contributed by the other authors, but because the 364 economists were the backbone of the institutions of learning at the time – as is noted in the chapter by Tim Congdon. The 364, and like-minded academics, taught nearly all university undergraduates and taught the teachers who taught the sixth-formers. The comments I wish to make would be out of place in the usual Editorial Director's foreword to IEA publications, thus I am adding these comments to those of the other authors of this monograph who were, with one exception, already active in their careers by 1981.[2]

---

1 For the record the school was Marist College, Hull, now called St Mary's College.

2 The exception is David Laws, MP. David Laws and I are close in age. He read economics at King's College, Cambridge (a hotbed of the 364), at more or less the same time as I read economics at the University of Durham. As will become clear,

In this chapter, I discuss the way in which macroeconomics teaching in the early 1980s often ignored scarcity and prices. This was at the heart of the misunderstanding of the 1981 Budget. The teaching of macroeconomics in the UK is much more thorough today, introducing in the mainstream textbooks approaches that deal properly with the problem of scarcity and the impact of changes in demand and supply on prices.

Some reflections up to 1982

For five years, we were taught microeconomics impeccably at school. We began, as many economics courses still do today, with the economic choices of Robinson Crusoe; the idea of capital arising from forgone consumption; and the importance of supply, demand, costs and prices in determining the allocation of resources. This was then extended to a world of free trade and comparative advantage. From an early stage, we were taught to think logically from a set of assumptions, through a chain of reasoning, to conclusions that could be derived from the assumptions. This mode of teaching provided me with an understanding of how markets work and reinforced an instinctive belief in a market economy. The teaching of economics was reinforced by the small amount of economic history that we covered in the history syllabus, dealing with the Industrial Revolution and related issues.

Much of the macroeconomics of so-called national income determination did not make sense in that context. It seemed to be

the 'economics with prices' that I read at Durham had little in common with the thinking of the 364. I remain grateful that a dropped A-level grade led me north, rather than south, to university.

taught in a box separate from the rest of economics. There was no mention of scarcity and none of prices. Particular issues such as unemployment or inflation were generally well taught but, when it was all put together in the so-called Keynesian cross diagram, it did not seem to make sense. Later I was to discover that what I had been learning, macroeconomics without prices, was the macroeconomics of the 364.

Against the tide

I was also aware that there was considerable opposition to the 1981 Budget within the parliamentary Conservative Party and also in its rank-and-file membership. This opposition was spread widely among people who were generally anti-Thatcher because they were pro-Heath (and/or pro-EU integration); among patrician Tories who had a genuine sympathy for the unemployed and who thought that incomes policy and lower interest rates might help them; among people who had become unemployed or who had their own businesses and who had been hard hit; and among party members with no particular views, in the areas suffering most from recession and who felt that something was going wrong somewhere. It seemed that the majority of the party at that time was openly hostile to, suspicious of or unable to articulate a clear justification for nearly all the policies of the 1979–83 Conservative government.

This is not surprising – the justification for the policies was necessarily abstract and the benefits of the policies seemed a long way off. That the 1981 Budget was implemented in a democracy with no external constraints (such as those imposed by the IMF on Denis Healey in 1976–79 or those imposed on countries preparing for EMU in the late 1990s) is a real testament to the intellectual conviction of a small number of politicians and their advisers.

I too was dissatisfied with the Conservative government. At some stage in 1980/81, prompted by what I had learnt about markets, I had written a letter to Margaret Thatcher asking her why she had not cut public spending as she had promised to do in 1979. I received a detailed reply, but one that made it pretty clear that there were not going to be significant spending cuts in the short run. It is of interest that, if the electorate in 1979 believed it had a contract with the government, an important aspect of that contract was that the government would cut spending and taxes. This part of the contract was never delivered. The 1981 Budget was, however, an overt expression of two other aspects of the contract between the electorate and the government being delivered – the desire to control public finances and the desire to defeat inflation through monetary policy.

From the perspective of public choice economics it might appear surprising that the government chose to fulfil these two aspects of its contract with the electorate but not the first. By cutting taxes and spending there would have been gainers and losers and the gainers would have been natural Conservative supporters. Yet it was difficult to identify immediate gainers from the process of restoring fiscal responsibility and reducing inflation – the gainers here were future generations. Did Thatcher and Howe act purely in the interests of the country with no thought whatsoever for their personal interests in the pursuit of this policy?[3] As a young idealist I assumed that politicians were generally motivated by principle.

---

3   Thatcher and Howe did, of course, retain power, but whether this was a result of the long-run success of their policies or because the alternative was unelectable is a moot point.

Economics with prices

From 1982 I was an undergraduate at Durham University. The big difference between 'macroeconomics' at Durham and macroeconomics taught in many other universities was that there was nothing explicitly identified as macroeconomics at Durham. The term was never used. And the decision not to use the term was deliberate. Issues such as unemployment and recession were analysed in the same way as microeconomic problems. Distortions or stickiness in relative prices were the generally identified causes of recessions and unemployment. The role of money was analysed explicitly. The consequences of policy changes such as a reduction in the fiscal deficit caused by an increase in taxes, as in the 1981 Budget, were rigorously thought through.

According to the 'economics without prices' of the 364 the £4 billion rise in taxes in the 1981 Budget would lead to a fall in national income due to a fall in aggregate demand. 'Economics with prices' looks at the issue more deeply. What happens as a result of the £4 billion reduction in the size of the deficit? The government can reduce the amount that it borrows from investors in financial markets, who have more money to invest in private sector projects or to spend on consumption. What are the second-round effects? What would happen to interest rates if government borrowing from the markets were reduced? What would happen to the exchange rate if interest rates fell? What would be the consequences for other aspects of economic activity of those changes in interest rates and the exchange rate? What would be the impact on employment of a fall in real wages if consumption fell in some sectors as a result of the tax rise? In short, we had to analyse the processes that could lead to 'crowding out' of private sector activity when the government increased its deficit and which could lead to increased private sector activity when the government decreased its deficit.

If we were to conclude that a £4 billion reduction in taxes would cause a £4 billion reduction in national income (plus a bit more because of the multiplier effect) then our assumptions about the rigidity of prices and of changes in resource allocation when prices changed would have to be made explicit. The analysis was rigorous – not necessarily mathematical, but rigorous.

Indeed, one lecture by Richard Morley involved diagram after diagram and ended with the statement 'That is the justification for Geoffrey Howe's 1981 Budget and why the 364 economists are wrong to say that there is no theoretical justification for it'.[4]

A number of IEA papers were part of a long and broad reading list, but it is worth mentioning that Friedman's *Counter Revolution in Monetary Theory* was among them. In *Counter Revolution*, Friedman cites evidence from the USA that fiscal policy had little impact on economic activity whereas monetary policy did. This evidence was from two episodes in the USA in the late 1960s (see Friedman and Goodhart, 2003: 80, 81[5]). This conclusion, translated across to the UK, would mean that the 1981 Budget would not send Britain deeper into recession, and it accords with 'Morleynomics'. A £4 billion increase in taxes reduces the budget deficit. This reduces the equilibrium level of interest rates and the exchange rate (or a combination of both, depending on

---

4   At this stage, I would like to mention that the main course lecturer was Richard Morley and my main tutors were Denis O'Brien and Di Sanderson. No permanent lecturers in the department at Durham signed the letter. One of the Durham signatories (see Appendix) was not in the Department of Economics, the other was a temporary lecturer.

5   *The Counter Revolution in Monetary Theory* was first published in 1970. The reference here is to the latest reprint.

assumptions relating to the movement of capital). This should lead to some combination of increased investment and/or consumption and/or exports and/or substitution of imports. This replaces the lost consumption arising from the tax increase. Now it is possible for these things not to happen, but that would require assumptions about sticky prices and strong assumptions about the responsiveness of demand and supply to prices. The evidence to support those assumptions should be provided by those who make them.

Economics without prices

In most of the institutions of higher learning, the above approach to macroeconomics would not have been taken.[6] Some time between summer 1982 and 1984, I saw a television programme investigating the early Thatcher years. Part of the programme showed an economics tutorial from Queen Mary College, London.[7] The tutor showed his tutees how national income would fall as a result of the Thatcher/Howe policies, using the Keynesian cross diagram. The message was simple: taxes are a 'withdrawal' from national income and an increase in taxes leads to an increase in withdrawals and a fall in national income. The message on how to raise national income was also straightforward – reduce withdrawals (most obviously taxes) or increase 'injections' (most obvi-

---

6   This might explain why nearly all City economists simply did not believe that inflation could be the result of the Lawson money supply boom of 1987/88.

7   I believe the tutor was Maurice Peston. It is coincidental that he is a contributor to this monograph, though not coincidental that he was one of the 364 economists. No specific criticism is intended: this tutorial could have taken place at almost any university in the country. I have no idea what issues and qualifications of the model were discussed off-screen.

ously government spending).[8] Relative prices and relative scarcity of economic resources were not mentioned.

This approach to economics, typical of the macroeconomic teaching of the time, was 'economics without prices' and 'economics without scarcity'. It is quite clear that there were unemployed economic resources in 1981. This made the theories that predicted that a £4 billion fiscal tightening would lead to a fall in national income so plausible. But it is because the theories were so intuitively plausible that it is important that their predictions should be tested. Intuitive plausibility is not a good test of a theory and it is not the job of academics merely to teach plausible ideas. In reality, though, the fact that 'economics without prices' and without scarcity was being taught frequently remained hidden from view because alternative ideas were not given an appropriate airing.

The most common textbook used at the time would have been Lipsey's *An Introduction to Positive Economics* (Lipsey, 1979). There are several chapters in the book on what is described as 'The Determination of National Income'. Conclusions such as 'A rise in the taxation, saving or import functions raises the aggregate withdrawals function and lowers equilibrium national income' (p. 500) are common (stated in bold and not qualified). Indeed, further discussion of the issue includes points such as 'National income theory predicts that the correct response to the Depression of the 1930s was to encourage firms, households and governments to

8   I recall one other point made in the television programme, which is of passing interest given that the IEA published on bus re-regulation six months ago (Hibbs, 2005). An academic (I am not sure whether or not this was also Maurice Peston) complained that the deregulation of buses was leading to the regrettable consequence of bus routes not being determined any longer by the traditional method of democratic processes but rather by undemocratic market forces.

spend and not to save[9] ... The suffering and misery of that unhappy decade would have been greatly reduced had those in authority known even as much economics as is contained in this chapter' (p. 501). David Laidler's criticisms of fiscal demand management are described as 'extreme' (p. 564).[10] There is a chapter right at the end of the book which pays a little attention to aggregate supply curves. That chapter is entitled 'Policy Issues and Debates'.[11] These policy issues and debates are, however, fundamental to the determination of national income, which, in the main section on this subject, is assumed to be determined only by demand, in turn determined by 'injections' of government spending, consumption and exports and 'withdrawals' of taxes, saving and imports. Keynes himself (Keynes, 1936) was much more careful to spell out the assumptions on which his analysis was based than his followers were.[12]

As it happens, even if we make the assumptions that many of the 364 were implicitly making, the 1981 Budget could still have been a pretty shrewd move. At the time, British industry was struggling to adjust to high real interest rates (caused by counter-inflationary monetary policy) and a high real exchange rate (caused by the same policy as well as by the production of North Sea oil). If reduced government borrowing reduces real interest rates and reduces the real exchange rate for a given monetary policy stance, the impact of the 1981 Budget would be to move the level

---

9   It should be noted that government 'saving' includes policies such as raising taxes – thus reducing borrowing.

10 Specifically, Lipsey states 'we cannot go into these extreme views here' – presumably owing to lack of space in an 810-page book.

11 This chapter is 26 pages compared with 123 pages on the 'circular flow of national income'.

12 Though how the title 'General Theory' for Keynes's work is justified has always escaped me – Keynes seems to claim that a special case is general and that the general case is special.

of real interest rates and the exchange rate closer to the levels that prevailed before the counter-inflationary monetary policy began. This could have helped a rigid economy adjust to the difficulties caused by a tight monetary policy.[13] Given their own assumptions, the 364 may well have been wrong about the impact of the 1981 Budget, but it is not clear how any of this could be analysed using their own toolkit. Economics without prices was an inadequate toolkit even for analysing Keynesian policies under Keynesian assumptions – as today's Keynesians would understand.

The possibility that there might be issues even more important than the problem of recession did not even seem to cross the minds of most economics teachers of the time. In the five years to 1979 the price level had doubled and the national debt had also doubled. Institutions investing in the gilt market had gone on 'strike' in the late 1970s, demanding ever higher interest rates, and also gilts with special conditions attached to reduce the risk of inflation to investors. If the Thatcher/Howe approach had failed to control the government deficit then investors might well have lost all confidence in any future UK government controlling it. The possibility of default or ever higher rates of inflation devaluing the debt in real terms would have become priced into the interest rates at which institutions were willing to lend. The social consequences of accelerating inflation and/or government debt default would have been far more serious than those from a temporary rise in unemployment.

It might be thought that those involved with economic policy-making would pay no attention to teachers of economics. Regrettably, the economic establishment in the civil service

---

13   Better still might have been a £4 billion reduction in government spending.

shared identical views. The 500-equation Treasury model of the economy at the time had no proper treatment of money and no equation for the relationship between real wages and employment. The intellectual courage of the originators, executors and promoters of the 1981 Budget had to be sufficient to take on virtually the whole of the established UK economics profession. 'Macroeconomics without prices' seemed to be the natural framework for the profession.

Lessons for today

My contention is that the 364 economists were badly misguided. Perhaps more importantly, academics of the day were misguiding others through a mode of teaching macroeconomics which, in effect, ignored prices and scarcity. It is simply not sufficient to say that because there was unemployment, scarcity and price adjustments were not relevant. Markets are not as simple as that. Labour is not a homogenous quantity and thus, even when there is unemployment, changes in wages affect employment and vice versa. The two mistakes of this form of macroeconomics, ignoring scarcity and ignoring prices, are reinforced by the fundamental error of treating aggregate variables as homogenous. Much that is relevant about economic systems is overlooked when we aggregate and treat factors of production as homogenous. In this section I ask whether these problems with economics teaching still exist today and also refer back to the politics of the 1981 Budget.

Macroeconomics teaching today

Students today receive a much more sophisticated diet of macroeconomics. In a typical textbook (for example, Begg et al., 1997[14]) there will still be a chapter or two on 'national income determination'. Assumptions are made much more explicit, however. Indeed, in the closing paragraph of the chapter on national income determination in Begg et al., it states, 'In this chapter we have focused on the short run before prices and wages have time to adjust' (p. 349 of the 1997 edition). The view that was the antithesis of the view of the 364, that it is only monetary policy which determines 'aggregate demand' and that in the long run monetary policy only influences prices and not supply, receives a fair treatment. Similarly the idea that tightening or loosening fiscal policy may have no impact on aggregate demand and supply because of the crowding-out effects of changes in interest rates or the exchange rate is also well treated. Ideas such as Ricardian equivalence are covered (indeed, it is given a two-page box all to itself, entitled 'Do tax cuts work?'). There is a proper, considered, theoretical and empirical treatment of the subject, even if one does not agree with the conclusions.

Miles and Scott (2002) is a basic textbook entitled *Macroeconomics*. In this book, there are as many references to Friedman as to Keynes. Only three pages are devoted to Keynesian national income models, and most of this text explains the models in terms of how they deviate from a neo-classical model. Again, assumptions are made explicit and this provides a much better base for teaching than the popular textbooks of the 1980s.

Austrian economists may well complain that consideration of aggregate quantities distorts our whole understanding of how the economy works. Some monetarists may complain that

14 I have used the fifth edition, printed in 1997, to demonstrate that a sounder approach has been around for a few years now.

money is not given thorough treatment. Also, the authors of the textbooks to which I have referred in this section are broadly 'Keynesian' in outlook. Nevertheless, most supporters of the 1981 Budget cannot really complain that a basic toolkit is not now provided to students of economics to analyse properly events such as the 1981 Budget.

Are there different areas of economics where teaching is poor?

If I were to identify one area of economics where teaching is as poor as the teaching of macroeconomics was 25 years ago, it would relate to the concept of 'market failure'. A typical approach would be as follows. The concept of perfect competition and a perfect market would be introduced in a microeconomics course. The assumptions would be spelt out in detail. The way in which those assumptions do not hold would then be discussed, thus leading to the concept of 'market failure'. The course would then go on to show how government can respond to 'market failure' by taking actions that would lead services to be delivered so that marginal social cost would equal marginal social benefit and so on.

There are several weaknesses in this approach. The first is that, in the absence of a perfect market, there are undiscovered opportunities for improving welfare. The whole point of a market economy, however, is to discover such opportunities and, if they are undiscovered, they cannot be discovered by government. In other words, if there is not a perfect market, the government would not know what the outcome of the perfect market would have been and therefore cannot achieve such an outcome through intervention. The second weakness is that public choice economics is rarely considered explicitly. Government cannot correct market failure because it is itself imperfect. Governments fail. Governments have imperfect information. Governments impose social costs. Governments do not respond omnisciently and beneficently but can often act to maximise the welfare of specific voter groups, politicians and bureaucrats. Unlike markets, governments are not constrained by freedom of contract.

The problem with teaching in this area is very similar to the problem of macroeconomic teaching 25 years ago. Markets are not adequately analysed and the assumptions that governments have perfect information and act without regard to the interests of voter groups, politicians and bureaucrats often remain hidden from the view of the student. Once these assumptions are made explicit, and once public choice economics and Austrian notions of competition are integrated properly into teaching, one can have a serious, rigorous debate about the best approach to dealing with specific economic policy problems. Today, like the relationship between fiscal and monetary policy and the idea of crowding out in the 1970s and early to mid-1980s, public choice economics, Austrian ideas of competition theory, government failure and market-generated solutions to problems of so-called 'market failure' receive occasional mentions when they should be fully integrated into the exposition of the subject.

As a result of this, it is rare to find intelligent graduates who believe in free markets who do not then go on to say, 'But we need the government to intervene to correct market failures.'

So, could we have another misconceived letter from 364 disgruntled economists? While such a letter on a macroeconomic issue is unlikely in the near future, the teaching of microeconomics, though generally rigorous, misses the crucial features mentioned above.[15] If we were to take a policy proposal such as school choice or privatisation of health insurance, one could certainly imagine a letter from 364 economists worded roughly as follows:

> We the undersigned do not believe that there is any justification for the policies that are being followed. They are based on a naive belief that markets work perfectly. There is no theoretical justification for the view that the policies being followed will improve education and health outcomes. Problems such as information asymmetries and external costs and benefits suggest that markets will fail to provide the optimal outcome.

Such a letter would make similar mistakes to the 1981 letter. Issues that are fundamental (in this case public choice economics and a misplaced view about market failure) are marginalised and underlying assumptions (for example, that of a perfect government providing education) are not spelt out and tested.

In conclusion, the letter from the 364 economists to *The Times* reflected economic thinking and teaching in the UK at that time. Thinking and teaching paid insufficient attention to more rigorous ideas and alternative theories were often not properly explained to students. Fortunately, things have changed, at least with regard to the teaching of macroeconomics.

---

15 The teaching of subjects where the syllabus contains elements of economics but where the syllabus is designed and taught by non-economists is often poor in the UK but I regard this as a separate issue. Topics such as the environment and certain aspects of economics that underpin law fall into this category – 'do-it-yourself economics' is rampant.

References

Begg, D. K. H., S. Fischer and R. Dornbusch (1997), *Economics*, 5th edn, Maidenhead: McGraw Hill.

Friedman, M. and R. Friedman (1980), *Free to Choose*, London: Secker and Warburg.

Friedman, M. and C. A. E. Goodhart (2003), *Money, Inflation and the Constitutional Position of the Central Bank*, IEA Readings 57, London: Institute of Economic Affairs.

Hibbs, J. (2005), *The Dangers of Bus Re-regulation*, Occasional Paper 137, London: Institute of Economic Affairs.

Keynes, J. M. (1936), *The General Theory of Employment Interest and Money*, London: Macmillan.

Lipsey, R. G. (1979), *An Introduction to Positive Economics*, 5th edn, London: Weidenfeld & Nicolson.

Miles, D. and A. Scott (2002), *Macroeconomics: Understanding the wealth of nations*, Chichester: Wiley.

7 ECONOMIC POLICY IN THE EARLY 1980S: WERE THE 364 WRONG?
David Laws

Introduction

My memories of the economic controversies of the early 1980s are still very clear today, if inevitably impressionistic. This was a time of acute economic turmoil, even crisis, when the political debate in Britain was dominated by our short- and long-term economic problems. As a teenager, I was both fascinated and disturbed by the economic turbulence that I witnessed. Britain seemed to be locked into a long-term economic decline, but the short-term crisis in the economy seemed to be even more dramatic and frightening, and to threaten a breakdown in the economic and social order of the country.

Unemployment was on the rise, increasing from 5.8 per cent in early 1980 to 12 per cent by late 1983. The economy had fallen into a sharp recession, with overall output falling at an annual rate of up to 4 per cent, and with a shocking 9 per cent decline in manufacturing output in 1980. Interest rates had soared to 17 per cent, inflation had risen to a peak of around 22 per cent, and the pound had risen to levels that were putting an unbearable squeeze on the traded goods sector.

Meanwhile, the government seemed wedded to a commitment to reduce the growth of various obscure monetary aggregates – a commitment that they seemed notably unable to deliver.

The overwhelming public sentiment that I recall from this period was that while Britain had been trapped in a long-term economic decline, the policies of the post-1979 Conservative government were making matters worse rather than better, and threatening the social cohesiveness of the whole nation.

This impression, formed from the media and from the dire statistics that were available each month, was reinforced by the first-hand experiences of my father, reported back to me on a regular basis. My father worked in the City of London, lending money to manufacturing companies in the North and the Midlands. He visited these firms on a regular, monthly, basis, and I was influenced by his strong view that government policies were 'cutting into industrial muscle, and not just fat'.

At Cambridge University, Professor Kaldor was making similar criticisms at the time. 'You do not cure a man of a cold by exposing him naked in the outdoors in the middle of a snowstorm' was his assessment of the effectiveness of government policy.

My fascination for politics led inevitably to a desire to study economics. In the early 1980s, no other subject seemed of any great relevance to the political debate.

The state of economic debate seemed confused at best. I recall my bafflement at reading the definition of 'economics' in my first textbook in Lesson 1 of my A-level economics course: 'economics is the science of allocating scarce resources between alternative, competing, uses'. This seemed to me an astonishing definition in an age of surplus resources – not least labour. Unemployment had already reached the shocking total of 3 million people, and – as in the 1930s – the challenge seemed to be to make use of plentiful resources rather than allocating scarce resources between alternative uses.

Cambridge in the early 1980s

My interest in economics and in politics led to the decision to study economics at university, and this led on to Cambridge, and to King's College. It was in the Faculty of Economics in Cambridge, in 1981, that the famous letter from 364 economists was drafted.

King's was not only the most beautiful of the Cambridge colleges, but it had the most distinguished reputation in economics – largely as the college of John Maynard Keynes. It was the obvious destination for a young man who was passionate about economics and instinctively sceptical about the government's macroeconomic management.

King's in 1984 was not quite the economics powerhouse of the 1930s. There was a sense of faded glory. But many of the signatories of the letter of 364 economists to *The Times* in 1981 were from the college. Anthony Giddens, Paul Ryan, James Trevithick and John Wells tutored me at King's, and all signed the letter. The letter was also signed by the great (Lord) Richard Kahn (a close colleague of Keynes, and a contemporary link to the world of the 'General Theory'), by the impish Lord Kaldor, and by the brilliant, unpredictable and charming Professor Wynne Godley – all these were fellows of King's.

Lord Kahn would still occasionally meet undergraduates in his rooms in the college. These seemed untouched (certainly undusted) from the days of the General Theory, and one would have been only mildly surprised to find Mr Keynes himself, lounging in one of the worn sofas by the window, in the half-light of an autumn evening.

Lord Kaldor would occasionally attend meetings of the King's College economics group. He would contribute some magisterial and totally impractical policy proposal ('The problem of the

British economy is the City. And the only answer to the City is ... dynamite!'). Then he would fall asleep a few minutes into the presentation by some enthusiastic undergraduate, waking just before the end of the meeting to share some anecdote from the Treasury of the 1960s.

But in spite of the presence of the Two 'Ks', as Kahn and Kaldor were known, it would be wrong to think that in 1984 there was a universal 'left-wing' Keynesian consensus in King's College, and indeed in Cambridge University.

It was not only that a lot of the new economic thinking in the 1980s was being driven by the 'neo-classical' economists from the USA, nor that the pamphlets of the Institute of Economic Affairs had begun to circulate in the university (though more in the guise of straw men designed to be demolished). There was a recognition that Britain's economic problems were in part a product of the breakdown, the failure, of the post-war Keynesian consensus. James Callaghan, Labour's prime minister from 1976 to 1979, had warned several years before that traditional Keynesian economics could work only by injecting ever more inflation into the economic system. There was also an acceptance on the centre ground of the political debate that for too long Britain's economy had been held back by over-mighty unions, inefficient nationalised industries and by a failure to face up to the economic facts of life.

I regarded myself as broadly opposed to the government's macroeconomic policies, as did most undergraduates, but I remember refusing to sign a petition supporting the miners' strike of the time, led by Arthur Scargill, when it was pushed in front of me on my first day at the university in 1984. Scepticism about the government's macroeconomic policies was not the same as opposition to their wider economic reforms.

There certainly was not, however, any acceptance in Cambridge that 'monetarism', as a macroeconomic policy, was effective, and it was this critique which lay behind the letter from the 364 economists in 1981. The 1981 letter was rather vague about which policies were to be preferred to the existing 'monetarist' policy. It claimed simply that 'there are alternative policies' and that 'the time has come to reject monetarist policies'. It was presumably rather easier to unite 364 economists around such generalities than around a coherent alternative strategy.

In 1981, opposition to 'monetarist policies' was not a fringe occupation. The obsession with targeting and controlling 'monetary aggregates' seemed like an impractical expression of ideological commitment, rather than practical economics or politics. There was controversy over which aggregates to target. There was poor performance in targeting the money supply. There was scepticism over whether monetary growth was really worth targeting – Kaldor strikingly compared monetary targeting with trying to make a patient better by targeting his temperature, rather than the causes of the disease.

Finally, monetarism seemed to have contributed to driving up interest rates and the real exchange rate to astonishing levels: 17 per cent interest rates imposed a heavy burden on businesses and households. Just as dangerously, high interest rates and (allegedly) the increasing production of North Sea oil drove the real exchange rate through the roof.

It was the high exchange rate which did so much damage to manufacturing industry, and which drove up unemployment. Between early 1980 and Q1 1981, the real exchange rate rose by some 15 per cent. In early 1981, the real exchange rate was 36 per cent higher than its 1990 trade-weighted level.

An assessment of the 364

There were two central criticisms in the letter of the 364 economists, and it is perhaps worth considering these. The central criticism was point (b) in the letter – that 'present policies will deepen
the depression, erode the industrial base of the economy, and
threaten its social and political stability'. No definition is given of
'present policies', so it is difficult to guess how extensive a critique
of the Howe/Thatcher strategy this is meant to be.

The other criticism, put in point (a) of the letter, seems more
specific: '... there is no basis in economic theory or supporting
evidence for the Government's belief that by deflating demand
they will bring inflation permanently under control and thereby
induce an automatic recovery in output and employment'.

Although it is true that unemployment went on rising, and
manufacturing output struggling, for many more years, it is also
true that soon after the letter was sent the recession ended, and
the economy started to grow again: this can hardly have been
what the 364 expected.

Why were they wrong? One reason is surely that they were
obsessed with the (superficially Keynesian) view that only fiscal
policy could work to end a recession. For some Keynesians, cuts
in interest rates were ineffective – 'pushing on a string', as it
was described. Only a fiscal boost, on this view, could end the
recession, even though there was already a forecast 6 per cent
public sector borrowing requirement. But Geoffrey Howe was
seeking not merely to reduce public borrowing but to 'rebalance'
economic policy. The tax changes were designed to 'enable us to
achieve our monetary objectives without having to face intoler-
ably high interest rates'. Interest rates were cut by 2 per cent on
Budget day, bringing them down to 12 per cent – fully 5 per cent

below the 1980 peak of 17 per cent. This was in spite of monetary growth running well above target.

The decline in interest rates at last began to bring down the exchange rate, and by the end of 1980 the pound had fallen back by 10–15 per cent from its early 1980 peak. So, alongside a fiscal tightening, there was a substantial monetary policy easing. This seems to have been ignored by the 364, or possibly they had not anticipated – perhaps understandably – the large decline in the exchange rate throughout 1981.

Given the circumstances at the time, this rebalancing of fiscal and monetary policy looks quite sensible. But it was far more controversial at the time, not least for economists wedded to the power of fiscal activism. The 1981 letter was therefore wrong to predict a deepening of the recession, and as such it has been widely derided, not least by those who were its principal targets.

Today, there is much less confidence in the power of fiscal activism, and a much greater belief in the power of monetary policy. There is also a clear understanding and acknowledgement of the interaction of fiscal and monetary policy.

The early 1980s are also seen, more generally, as a time when Britain confronted some of the causes of its long-term economic decline, and introduced a range of economic policies to reverse this decline. These would include: greater budgetary discipline; a commitment to low and stable inflation; a reduction in union power; privatisation of state-run enterprises; and an unwillingness to subsidise or tolerate economic inefficiency. But a high price was paid in the early 1980s for breaking the back of British inflation, and for 'shaking out' inefficient businesses.

Unemployment hit one of its highest levels in British history, and remained high for many years. Some of those who lost their jobs never worked again – claiming long-term incapacity benefit instead. The social costs of this breakdown in employment scarred large parts of the country for many years to come. British manufacturing industry remained anaemic, and its output performance was one of the worst in the developed world. Meanwhile, monetary policy came to be implemented more pragmatically, and the central role of monetary targets was quietly shelved.

Was the macroeconomic policy of the early 1980s the right one? Was it a necessary part of the restoration of broader economic sanity, or an ideologically driven cold shower which would have been even more damaging had the overshooting of monetary aggregates not been ignored? Was the government lucky in 1980 that the exchange rate crumbled, ushering in a substantial monetary easing, or was this the effect of a well-judged rebalancing of policy?

The 364 economists who signed the Statement on Economic Policy in 1981 are now widely regarded as having lost the economic 'war'. The broad economic policies of the 1979–97 Tory administrations are seen to have turned around the British economy. But the definitive history of the 'macroeconomic battle' of 1980–82, with all its potential counter-factuals, is surely yet to be written.

THE 1981 BUDGET – A TURNING POINT FOR UK MACROECONOMIC THINKING
Derek Scott

The few against the establishment

If they had been right about the 1981 Budget and its effect on the British economy, a letter from one economist would have been enough, but the fact that 364 economists signed the letter drafted in Cambridge by Professors Hahn and Neild should have been sufficient warning to anyone not involved. It may be a matter of temperament, but if all the most eminent of any profession – be they economists, teachers, churchmen or chief constables – are lined up behind a proposition, it sets alarm bells ringing in my mind.

That's not to say I had the clarity of thought of those individuals within No. 10 – particularly the estimable Alan Walters – or the Treasury, who were responsible for the 1981 Budget: far from it. I had certainly learnt a great deal from my time as special adviser to Denis Healey during the Callaghan government, but not quite enough by 1981. And looking from today's perspective it is obvious that the Wilson and Callaghan governments certainly made some big mistakes (and some of these were clear enough at the time), but it would be interesting to see how some of their current successors would have succeeded in those circumstances: a clapped-out economy, two huge hikes in oil prices, an unreformed trade union movement and a party that was slipping into madness, led by the likes of Tony Benn (it is amazing how in some circles this man is regarded as a 'great parliamentarian' when at the peak of his power he did all he could to make Labour MPs accountable to the party caucus – but that is another story).

Today, it is very difficult to regain the perspective of 25 years ago. This was brought home to me in 2005 when I participated in a seminar at Churchill College, Cambridge, attended by politicians, civil servants, advisers and commentators with experience of the 1974–79 Labour government and the first Thatcher administration, as well as several young graduates and undergraduates who were too young to have had any first-hand memories of the years we were discussing. In many ways I think it was easier in the late 1970s to get into the skins of politicians of the 1930s than it is today, for those not around at the time, to grasp what it was like a quarter of a century ago and hence understand the shock caused in many circles by the 1981 Budget.

But in other respects the final phases of the 1974–79 government have the look of inevitability about them, at least in hindsight: the culmination of a series of failed attempts by governments of both parties to put the British economy in order, with the final chapter opening with Edward Heath in 1971 (or arguably the defeat of 'In Place of Strife' in 1969) and ending in the Winter of Discontent. During this period, generally decent and well-meaning politicians in both parties grappled with problems within some very real economic and political constraints. It is very easy to forget this today; and Patrick Minford made a very wise observation about this period when he said that 'it was necessary to change everything before you could change anything'.

That's essentially what happened during the 1980s, but it was a messier business than it appears in hindsight. The intellectual basis for the change, from Sir Keith Joseph and others, had been germinating for a long time, but this would have been to no avail if events on the ground hadn't cried out for change: timing is very important in politics. Mrs Thatcher could have had the same views ten years earlier but it would have done her little good (in fact she seems to have had rather different views then). By the end of the 1970s the economic and political outlook had become so bleak that almost everyone recognised that something had to change, and this tide brought in Mrs Thatcher, but the response of the 364 economists showed how far there was to go in shifting the views of the economic establishment, and although the political tide had shifted, it required considerable political skill, guts and not a little luck to see through the necessary changes. The Thatcher revolution appears more inevitable in 2006 than it seemed at the time.

A lasting counter-revolution in thinking on macroeconomic policy

A 'new' approach

In some ways the 1981 Budget encapsulated the change, and if it had not gone through, Alan Walters and John Hoskyns (high priests of the new regime) would have resigned from No. 10. But its real significance was as part of a wider shift in the approach to economic policy that turned on its head much of the previous consensus. By the time Tony Blair entered Downing Street in 1997 there was again a great deal of common ground between the two main political parties on economic policy (at least between their two leaderships). It had taken quite some time, however, before the benefits of the changes encapsulated in 1981 were fully realised, not least because some of the most articulate proponents of the principles that underlay the 1981 Budget, including Nigel Lawson, lost their way.

This period was important for those of us who could not be described as in the vanguard in 1981. This was certainly the period, reinforced by more than a decade in the City, when my own economic views changed and clarified; but it was not until 1992, more than a decade later, that the jigsaw was finally put together, laying the foundations for an unprecedented period of economic growth and stability. The worry today is that some politicians seem to take this success for granted rather than trying to understand the conditions that made it possible.

The 1981 Budget was directed primarily at reducing the public sector borrowing requirement (PSBR) and bringing the Medium Term Financial Strategy (MTFS) back on course. The most comprehensive statement of the overall economic stance reflected in the 1981 Budget was made a few years later by Nigel Lawson, Financial Secretary to the Treasury in 1981, and author of the MTFS, when speaking as Chancellor of the Exchequer at the Mais Lecture in 1984.

The consensus for most of the post-war period was that macro-economic policy, in the form of demand management, was the key to stimulating growth and maintaining full employment (although it is possible to argue that it was only the 1959 and 1972 budgets which were aimed at reducing unemployment, otherwise fiscal policy was directed mainly at avoiding problems with the balance of payments and/or inflation). Meanwhile microeconomic policy – above all various measures of wage control – was the key to low inflation.

In 1984 Lawson asserted the exact opposite. He said that macroeconomic policy should be responsible for controlling inflation, and should have no role in stimulating growth or creating jobs. The other side of the coin was that microeconomic policy should be concerned with promoting economic growth and jobs, but should have no part in controlling inflation. Furthermore, Lawson argued that, within both the micro and macro areas, the key instruments of policy should change. The crucial macro instrument was not budgetary policy – the variation of taxation and public spending to prevent recessions – but monetary policy. Interest rates should be set to achieve low inflation, and that was the main macroeconomic responsibility of the Chancellor of the Exchequer. Elsewhere the private sector could be left to look after itself. This belief in market forces governed the supply side too. The government should accept no responsibility to help the market function successfully through intervention. Instead it should cease interfering with the market process wherever practicable. Deregulation and privatisation were the instruments by which this was to be achieved.

Lawson made another point. The reduced role for government was to be reflected in a gradual reduction in the share of tax and spending in GDP. Lower marginal tax rates would further increase the private sector's incentive to make the economy succeed. The notable thing was that, with a few caveats, most of this was accepted by Tony Blair when he gave his own Mais Lecture a decade after Lawson. Indeed, in some respects Blair went farther than Lawson. For example, on inflation he said it was not enough to say that inflation does no good for growth beyond the shortest of time horizons. Inflation, he emphasised, is bad for economic growth. To quote: '... temporary fluctuations in inflation – short term failings of macro-economic policy – can have permanent damaging effects on the ability of the economy to sustain high levels of output and jobs'.

The Treasury loses its way again

In the decade between these two Mais Lectures, however, those who had set the course in 1981 lost their way, or at least some of them did (Alan Walters never wavered, but he had left No. 10 and was less able to support the instincts of Mrs Thatcher), and one of them unfortunately happened to be Chancellor – Nigel Lawson. The monetary framework became confused and changed whenever it seemed convenient. Monetary aggregates were 'monitored' rather than targeted. The exchange rate came into greater prominence and so on. The result was that an excessive amount of reliance came to be placed on the judgement of the Chancellor. The medium-term framework was increasingly defined in virtually any way the Chancellor chose.

Most fundamentally there was a complete failure to appreciate the connection between microeconomic and macroeconomic policy: the very core of the shift in policy in the 1980s. By 1987 the fruits of the supply-side reforms to capital, product and labour markets were becoming apparent and the rise in anticipated rates of return was generating a rapid rise in investment expenditure by businesses and households. When this happens there is a rise in the equilibrium real rate of interest – the rate of interest that keeps the economy in some sort of overall balance. In order for the anticipated real rate of interest in Britain to be above the world rate it is necessary for investors to anticipate a fall in the exchange rate, and for this to happen it must have risen first to levels from which it is expected to decline. The correct response is to raise short-term interest rates and allow the currency to appreciate.

In pursuit of a 'stable' exchange rate, Lawson did the opposite: sterling was capped against the Deutschmark, interest rates were kept too low, the boom got out of hand, to be followed by the inevitable bust. Entry to the Exchange Rate Mechanism (ERM) only made things worse, and the British economy could only be put to right after sterling's exit in 1992.

Back on course: a new consensus on macroeconomic policy

Since 1992 the British economy has experienced a period of unprecedented growth and stability and a large measure of consensus among policy-makers. To that extent, just as the years between 1971 and 1979 can be seen as the last gasp of the economic attitudes that dominated the post-war decades, the period from 1981 to 1992 can be seen as an important turning point. The right course was set, but those in charge lost their bearings in the latter part of the 1980s. They recovered them later, but by that time their reputation for political competence had been lost and they were thrown out of office. Under Blair and Brown the same basic tenets were followed (at least for some time).

There are three main domestic factors behind Britain's economic success since 1992 (the relatively benign international background, particularly strong growth in the USA for most of the time, has been an important non-domestic factor): first, the supply-side reforms to labour, product and capital markets introduced by the Thatcher administration; second, the decisions taken by the Chancellor of the Exchequer, Norman Lamont, in the wake of the ERM shambles (whatever his mistakes before) to cut spending and raise taxes to put the public finances on a sound footing (in a sense restoring the 1981 Budget settlement); third, the decision of the incoming Labour government in 1997 to make the Bank of England independent (also building on the earlier framework set up by Lamont), which provided the framework that allowed the benefits of the earlier changes to be consolidated.

Are we now losing our way in microeconomic policy?

The problem is that when an economy has been performing well for a little while, politicians start taking it for granted and start undermining the very conditions that made it possible. That is the biggest threat in Britain. This threat manifests itself by policies leading to too much micro-management, excessive public expenditure and increased burdens from regulation and tax. This has happened before and not just in Britain. At the end of World War II, Ludwig Erhard laid the foundations for Germany's post-war economic miracle. He was an extraordinary man, but in his commitment to liberal economics he was very isolated in Germany and beyond (the British economy was being socialised at the very moment Erhard was taking Germany in the opposite direction). Gradually, however, his work was undermined by his colleagues and successors.

There is much that Britain and Germany could still learn from Erhard, particularly in the emphasis he placed on the role of the entrepreneur (so-called endogenous growth theory imputing an increased role for the government is moving in exactly the wrong direction) and on markets more generally. Erhard was opposed to the creation of a large welfare state and when he talked about the social market economy he made it very clear that the market was social, not that it needed to be made social. Over the years this has been forgotten and in too many countries, including Germany, the so-called European Social Model has become the antithesis of what Erhard introduced.

There are lessons for Britain too, not only in the importance of markets for efficiency, but in their social role: markets allow the outsiders, including the unemployed and new businesses, to get on the inside, and today liberalised markets would allow some of the poorest countries in the world to raise themselves up by participating fully in the international economy. This social aspect is usually ignored by the parties of the so-called 'left', which should be in favour of helping the underdog get on the ladder, but markets and society are two sides of the same coin, and this is perhaps a message that has been lost since 1981.

APPENDIX

The contents of the key documents are reprinted in this appendix. They include the original letter requesting signatures, the statement of economic policy to which the signatories were agreeing, with some comments by the authors of the letter soliciting signatures, the list of signatories and the government's response.

Letter requesting signatures

The letter requesting signatures, dated Friday, 13 March 1981, was signed by Professor F. H. Hahn and Professor R. R. Neild, printed on University of Cambridge, Faculty of Economics and Politics, notepaper. The letter read as follows:

Dear Colleague,
We believe that a large number of economists in British universities, whatever their politics, think the Government's present economic policies to be wrong and that, for the sake of the country – and the profession – it is time we all spoke up. We have therefore prepared the attached statement, cast in terms which we hope will command wide agreement.

We are sending it to one senior member of each British university. Our plan is to circulate the statement with the list of signatories to the Press within ten days.

Will you please bring the statement to the attention

of any of your present or past colleagues whom you think might wish to sign it, taking copies if that makes the task easier.

Please send the signed statements back in time to reach us by Monday 23rd March. Signatories should be confined to present and past teaching officers and equivalent staff.

Statement on economic policy

The signatories to the letter were signing up to a statement on economic policy which is reproduced below with the comments from the two Cambridge academics who organised the statement. This statement was also printed on University of Cambridge, Faculty of Economics and Politics, notepaper.

Statement on economic policy

The following statement on economic policy has been signed by 364 university economists in Britain, whose names are given on the attached list:

'We, who are all present or retired members of the economics staffs of British universities, are convinced that:

(a) there is no basis in economic theory or supporting evidence for the Government's belief that by deflating demand they will bring inflation permanently under control and thereby induce an automatic recovery in output and employment;

(b) present politics will deepen the depression, erode the

industrial base of our economy and threaten its social and political stability;

(c) there are alternative policies; and

(d) the time has come to reject monetarist policies and consider urgently which alternative offers the best hope of sustained recovery.'

Analysis
Those who signed include:
(a) 76 present or past professors;
(b) a majority of the Chief Economic Advisers to the Government since the war: Professor James Meade, Lord Roberthall, Sir Alec Cairncross, Sir Bryan Hopkin and Sir Fred Atkinson;
(c) the President; 9 of the Vice-Presidents, and the Secretary-General of the Royal Economic Society.

The statement was circulated as university terms were ending. The rates of response have therefore been influenced by when term ended, by how dispersed is the community of university teachers in the vacation, as well as by the climate of economic opinion in each university.

Origins
The statement was sent by us to one member of each university on 13 March with a covering letter which said:

'We believe that a large number of economists in British universities, whatever their politics, think the Government's present economic policies to be wrong and that, for the sake of the country – and the profession – it is time we all spoke up. We have therefore prepared the attached statement, cast

in terms which we hope will command wide agreement.'
   A copy of the letter is attached.

F H Hahn
R R Neild

List of signatories

The signatories include a number of prominent people in the economics profession or in government today. For example, they include the Governor of the Bank of England and one other current member of the Monetary Policy Committee, members of the House of Lords and several other notable leading British economists. The signatories also include a number of recent IEA authors and present members of the IEA Academic Advisory Council. The names have been checked against the published list of signatories; however, no checking has been undertaken to ensure that there were no errors in that original list.

Statement on economic policy: list of signatures

Aberdeen University
J. A. Cairns
Professor M. Gaskin
A. H. Harris
A. G. Kemp
P. D. Murphy
D. A. Newlands
Professor D. W. Pearce
R. Shaw

Bath University
Professor D. Collard
R. P. Kamat
P. Mosley

Birmingham University
R. E. Backhouse
R. Clarke
D. G. Dickinson

M. G. Kanbur
Professor M. A. King

Bradford University
Sir Fred Atkinson (Professor)
J. E. Dunworth
M. Wilkinson
P. R. D. Wilson

Bristol University
J. Beath
R. Berry
A. A. Brewer
J. Broome
M. J. Browning
Professor W. H. Buiter
M. Clarke
Professor A. S. Deaton
M. Irish
I. Jewitt
R. Lacomber
H. S. B. Rees
D. C. Webb
D. Winter
L. A. Winters

Cambridge University
T. Barker
I. Begg
V. Borooah

S. Brodersen
Professor G. Cameron
Professor D. Champernowne
K. Coutts
J. C. Craig
F. Cripps
D. A. Dawson
P. M. Deane
J. L. Eatwell
R. Evans
A. Giddens
Professor W. A. H. Godley
A. Goudie
Professor F. H. Hahn
J. Humphries
G. K. Ingham
R. C. Jobling
Lord Kahn (Professor)
Lord Kaldor (Professor)
S. M. Kanbur
M. Kumar
M. Landesmann
A. Lawson
Professor J. E. Meade
G. Meeks
D. E. Moggridge
B. Moore
H. Myoken
Professor R. R. Neild
P. Nolan

M. H. Pesaran
W. Peterson
R. van der Ploeg
Professor W. B. Reddaway
J. Rhodes
Sir Austin Robinson
    (Professor)
Professor J. Robinson
J. Rubery
P. Ryan
S. Smith
K. Starzec
A. Sutherland
R. Tarling
S. Treitereid
J. Trevithick
Professor H. A. Turner
T. W. Ward
M. R. Weale
J. R. Wells
C. Whitehead
F. Wilkinson

Cardiff, University College
C. Baber
D. Barry
J. S. Bennett
R. Blackmore
T. Boyns
B. Curry

Professor K. D. George
G. Harbour
G. C. Hockley
Professor Sir Bryan Hopkin
C. J. McKenna
R. McNabb
L. Mainwaring
S. Owen
M. Phelps
D. G. Rhys
J. Shorey
D. R. Thomas

City University
J. Ansar
N. Bosanquet
P. Cook
D. Gray
Professor C. D. Harbury
P. Holl
K. R. Kirton
T. E. Tutton

Dundee University
P. G. Chapman
A. A. Lonie
C. M. Lyntag
M. J. Tooze

Durham University
R. A. H. Middleton
P. A. Winston

Edinburgh University
M. Fransman
D. H. R. George
L. T. Oxley
G. C. Reid
C. J. Roberts
S. T. Sayer
Professor T. Vandome

Glasgow University
G. C. Abbott
P. B. Beaumont
N. G. Clark
M. W. Danson
J. Foster
Professor L. C. Hunter
C. Kay
J. L. Latham
W. F. Lever
D. Maclennan
R. G. Milne
E. R. Rado
L. Sirc
Professor A. S. Skinner
Professor A. Slaven

Hull University
Professor J. S. G. Wilson

Keele University
S. A. Hussain

Kent University
A. Carruth
M. A. H. Katouzian
M. T. Sinclair
W. Smith
Professor A. P. Thirlwall

Lancaster University
H. W. Armstrong
V. N. Balasubramanyam
J. Channon
R. W. Daniels
J. Fender
J. E. King
Professor A. I. Macbean
C. Macgregor-Reid
D. T. Nguyen
N. Oulton
D. J. Payne
P. Regan
M. B. Rose
R. Rothschild
P. N. Snowden
J. Taylor

Professor H. Townsend
P. M. Westall

Leeds University
Professor A. J. Brown
J. A. Chartres
H. J. Radice
J. S. Rothwell
Professor M. J. Surrey

Leicester University
D. X. Bhattacharyya
Professor P. M. Jackson

London University

  Birkbeck College
F. Atkins
M. Ball
R. Bennett
I. Brunskill
H. Davies
B. Fine
G. Kennally
Professor J. Muellbauer
Professor R. Portes
R. P. Smith
D. Snower
A. Spanos

Imperial College
S. C. Hall
H. Motamen
D. Shepherd
Professor Z. A. Silberston
R. N. Strange
J. N. Turk

London School of Economics
Professor A. B. Atkinson
Professor P. Dasgupta
J. Davidson
C. R. S. Dougherty
J. Le Grande
K. Klappholz
A. Marin
Professor M. Morishima
Professor S. J. Nickell
J. Sutton
Professor P. J. D. Wiles

Queen Mary College
R. J. Allard
J. S. Cubbin
Professor B. A. Curry
H. S. E. Gravelle
Professor M. H. Peston

University College
Lord Balogh

W. Corlett
C. Catephores
C. Heady
Professor P. D. Henderson
A. Markandya
M. Pemberton
K. Schott
Professor J. Spraos
M. Stewart
D. Ulph
R. Vaughan
D. Verry

Manchester University
Professor M. J. Artis
J. M. Currie
P. Devine
M. C. Kennedy
C. H. Kirkpatrick
P. F. Leeson
Professor J. S. Metcalf
T. Peach
W. Peters
D. L. Purdy
J. B. Slater
Professor I. Steedman
P. C. Stubbs

*National Institute for Economic
    and Social Research*
P. S. O'Brien

Newcastle University
A. R. Shah

Nottingham University
J. M. Bates
K. A. Ingersent
A. N. Jennings
Professor J. Mitchell
Professor J. R. Parkinson
Professor A. J. Rayner
G. V. Reed
Professor J. H. B. Tew
D. K. Whynes
R. J. Young

Oxford University
B. Banerjee
W. Beckerman
C. J. E. Bliss
Professor Sir Alec Cairncross
A. Graham
V. Joshi
M. C. Kaser
K. Mayhew
A. Oswald
Lord Roberthall

D. Robinson
B. C. Rosewell
Professor A. K. Sen

Queen's University (Belfast)
Professor R. D. G. Black

Reading University
Professor P. E. Hart

Sheffield University
R. Clarke
Professor G. Clayton
D. J. Goacher
D. Kitchin
R. Lawson
J. Peirson
S. G. Tebbutt

Southampton University
C. J. Hawkins
Professor K. Hilton
G. W. McKenzie
Professor G. E. Mizon
R. J. O'Brien
Professor D. C. Rowan

Stirling University
P. J. W. N. Bird
Professor C. V. Brown

M. S. Common
G. Evans
D. Ghosh
R. T. Hamilton
P. G. Hare
C. Normand
R. Shone

Strathclyde University
R. G. Brooks
Professor A. I. Clunies-Ross
K. Hancock
J. Sconller
P. Wanless

Sussex University
Professor T. Barna
P. Lesley Cook
P. Holmes
D. Hunt
Professor D. Winch

Swansea, University College
N. Baigent
D. Donneky
J. T. Harris
L. C. Hunt
I. Jeffries
H. C. Petith
D. E. L. Thomas

University of East Anglia
D. Bailey
Professor K. N. Bhaskar
S. W. Davies
M. Dietrich
A. E. B. Heading
Professor H. F. Lydall
Professor A. Parikh
Professor A. G. Schweinberger
J. T. Thoburn

University of Wales, Bangor
Chakravarty
J. Fletcher
E. P. Gardener
R. H. Gray
A. J. Hopkins
R. R. Mackay
Morrell
Professor J. R. S. Revell

University College of Wales,
    Institute of Science and
    Technology
N. F. B. Allington
P. R. Bridger
Professor Glyn Davies
J. W. Evans
G. M. Holmes
T. W. Taylor

D. R. Turner

Warwick University
J. Brack
P. Burridge
Professor K. Cowling
Professor A. G. Ford
M. Harrison
C. G. Hayden
N. J. Ireland
K. G. Knight
P. J. Law
D. Leech
Professor M. Miller
S. K. Nath
G. Renshaw
J. I. Round
B. Sadler
M. Salmon
A. Snell
Professor N. H. Stern
M. Stewart
P. Stoneman
P. A. Weller

York University
D. Austen-Smith
R. R. Barnett
P. Burrows
Professor C. H. Feinstein

K. Hartley	J. W. Posnett
J. P. Hutton	M. Sawyer
D. T. Jenkins	P. M. Solar
P. J. Lambert	J. Suckling
J. M. Malcolmson	G. B. Stafford
A. K. Maynard	R. B. Weir
D. S. Poskitt	Professor A. Williams

Government response

The following response was published by the government.

GOVERNMENT RESPONSE TO PETITION FROM 364
ACADEMIC ECONOMISTS
The Government has read with interest the four points to
which these 364 economists subscribe. The Government,
however, agree [*sic*] with the substantial school of
economists which do [*sic*] believe that there is a strong
connection between monetary growth and the rate of
inflation, and has itself set out its thinking on this in
evidence to the Treasury Select Committee. So far as output
and employment are concerned, the Government's supply
side policies have been designed with the objective of raising
both output and employment specifically in mind. Such
policies are directed in particular to fostering the more
effective working of market forces and the restoration of
incentive [*sic*]. But experience has shown that injections of
monetary demand can at best have limited effect, and are
ultimately counter-productive.

For these reasons, the Government totally disagrees
with the assertion that present policies will deepen the
depression and weaken the UK's industrial base. Countries
pursuing policies broadly of the kind being implemented
here are those with the strongest industrial base.

It is conspicuous that although the 364 economists assert that there are alternative policies, they are unable to specify any such agreed alternatives.

ABOUT THE IEA

The Institute is a research and educational charity (No. CC 235 351), limited by guarantee. Its mission is to improve understanding of the fundamental institutions of a free society with particular reference to the role of markets in solving economic and social problems.

The IEA achieves its mission by:

- a high-quality publishing programme
- conferences, seminars, lectures and other events
- outreach to school and college students
- brokering media introductions and appearances

The IEA, which was established in 1955 by the late Sir Antony Fisher, is an educational charity, not a political organisation. It is independent of any political party or group and does not carry on activities intended to affect support for any political party or candidate in any election or referendum, or at any other time. It is financed by sales of publications, conference fees and voluntary donations.

In addition to its main series of publications the IEA also publishes a quarterly journal, *Economic Affairs*.

The IEA is aided in its work by a distinguished international Academic Advisory Council and an eminent panel of Honorary Fellows. Together with other academics, they review prospective IEA publications, their comments being passed on anonymously to authors. All IEA papers are therefore subject to the same rigorous independent refereeing process as used by leading academic journals.

IEA publications enjoy widespread classroom use and course adoptions in schools and universities. They are also sold throughout the world and often translated/reprinted.

Since 1974 the IEA has helped to create a world-wide network of 100 similar institutions in over 70 countries. They are all independent but share the IEA's mission.

Views expressed in the IEA's publications are those of the authors, not those of the Institute (which has no corporate view), its Managing Trustees, Academic Advisory Council members or senior staff.

Members of the Institute's Academic Advisory Council, Honorary Fellows, Trustees and Staff are listed on the following page.

The Institute gratefully acknowledges financial support for its publications programme and other work from a generous benefaction by the late Alec and Beryl Warren.

Other papers recently published by the IEA include:

WHO, What and Why?

Transnational Government, Legitimacy and the World Health Organization
Roger Scruton
Occasional Paper 113; ISBN 0 255 36487 3
£8.00

The World Turned Rightside Up

A New Trading Agenda for the Age of Globalisation
John C. Hulsman
Occasional Paper 114; ISBN 0 255 36495 4
£8.00

The Representation of Business in English Literature

Introduced and edited by Arthur Pollard
Readings 53; ISBN 0 255 36491 1
£12.00

Anti-Liberalism 2000

The Rise of New Millennium Collectivism
David Henderson
Occasional Paper 115; ISBN 0 255 36497 0
£7.50

Capitalism, Morality and Markets

Brian Griffiths, Robert A. Sirico, Norman Barry & Frank Field
Readings 54; ISBN 0 255 36496 2
£7.50

A Conversation with Harris and Seldon

Ralph Harris & Arthur Seldon
Occasional Paper 116; ISBN 0 255 36498 9
£7.50

Malaria and the DDT Story

Richard Tren & Roger Bate
Occasional Paper 117; ISBN 0 255 36499 7
£10.00

A Plea to Economists Who Favour Liberty: Assist the Everyman

Daniel B. Klein
Occasional Paper 118; ISBN 0 255 36501 2
£10.00

The Changing Fortunes of Economic Liberalism

Yesterday, Today and Tomorrow
David Henderson
Occasional Paper 105 (new edition); ISBN 0 255 36520 9
£12.50

The Global Education Industry

Lessons from Private Education in Developing Countries
James Tooley
Hobart Paper 141 (new edition); ISBN 0 255 36503 9
£12.50

Saving Our Streams

The Role of the Anglers' Conservation Association in
Protecting English and Welsh Rivers
Roger Bate
Research Monograph 53; ISBN 0 255 36494 6
£10.00

Better Off Out?

The Benefits or Costs of EU Membership
Brian Hindley & Martin Howe
Occasional Paper 99 (new edition); ISBN 0 255 36502 0
£10.00

Buckingham at 25

Freeing the Universities from State Control
Edited by James Tooley
Readings 55; ISBN 0 255 36512 8
£15.00

Lectures on Regulatory and Competition Policy

Irwin M. Stelzer
Occasional Paper 120; ISBN 0 255 36511 X
£12.50

Misguided Virtue

False Notions of Corporate Social Responsibility
David Henderson
Hobart Paper 142; ISBN 0 255 36510 1
£12.50

HIV and Aids in Schools

The Political Economy of Pressure Groups and Miseducation
Barrie Craven, Pauline Dixon, Gordon Stewart & James Tooley
Occasional Paper 121; ISBN 0 255 36522 5
£10.00

The Road to Serfdom

The Reader's Digest *condensed version*
Friedrich A. Hayek
Occasional Paper 122; ISBN 0 255 36530 6
£7.50

Bastiat's *The Law*

Introduction by Norman Barry
Occasional Paper 123; ISBN 0 255 36509 8
£7.50

A Globalist Manifesto for Public Policy

Charles Calomiris
Occasional Paper 124; ISBN 0 255 36525 X
£7.50

Euthanasia for Death Duties

Putting Inheritance Tax Out of Its Misery
Barry Bracewell-Milnes
Research Monograph 54; ISBN 0 255 36513 6
£10.00

Liberating the Land
The Case for Private Land-use Planning
Mark Pennington
Hobart Paper 143; ISBN 0 255 36508 x
£10.00

IEA Yearbook of Government Performance 2002/2003
Edited by Peter Warburton
Yearbook 1; ISBN 0 255 36532 2
£15.00

Britain's Relative Economic Performance, 1870–1999
Nicholas Crafts
Research Monograph 55; ISBN 0 255 36524 1
£10.00

Should We Have Faith in Central Banks?
Otmar Issing
Occasional Paper 125; ISBN 0 255 36528 4
£7.50

The Dilemma of Democracy
Arthur Seldon
Hobart Paper 136 (reissue); ISBN 0 255 36536 5
£10.00

Capital Controls: a 'Cure' Worse Than the Problem?

Forrest Capie

Research Monograph 56; ISBN 0 255 36506 3

£10.00

The Poverty of 'Development Economics'

Deepak Lal

Hobart Paper 144 (reissue); ISBN 0 255 36519 5

£15.00

Should Britain Join the Euro?

The Chancellor's Five Tests Examined

Patrick Minford

Occasional Paper 126; ISBN 0 255 36527 6

£7.50

Post-Communist Transition: Some Lessons

Leszek Balcerowicz

Occasional Paper 127; ISBN 0 255 36533 0

£7.50

A Tribute to Peter Bauer

John Blundell et al.

Occasional Paper 128; ISBN 0 255 36531 4

£10.00

Employment Tribunals

Their Growth and the Case for Radical Reform

J. R. Shackleton

Hobart Paper 145; ISBN 0 255 36515 2

£10.00

Climate Alarmism Reconsidered

Robert L. Bradley Jr
Hobart Paper 146; ISBN 0 255 36541 1
£12.50

Government Failure: E. G. West on Education

Edited by James Tooley & James Stanfield
Occasional Paper 130; ISBN 0 255 36552 7
£12.50

Waging the War of Ideas

John Blundell
Second edition
Occasional Paper 131; ISBN 0 255 36547 0
£12.50

Corporate Governance: Accountability in the Marketplace

Elaine Sternberg
Second edition
Hobart Paper 147; ISBN 0 255 36542 X
£12.50

The Land Use Planning System

Evaluating Options for Reform
John Corkindale
Hobart Paper 148; ISBN 0 255 36550 0
£10.00

Economy and Virtue

Essays on the Theme of Markets and Morality
Edited by Dennis O'Keeffe
Readings 59; ISBN 0 255 36504 7
£12.50

Free Markets Under Siege

Cartels, Politics and Social Welfare
Richard A. Epstein
Occasional Paper 132; ISBN 0 255 36553 5
£10.00

Unshackling Accountants

D. R. Myddelton
Hobart Paper 149; ISBN 0 255 36559 4
£12.50

The Euro as Politics

Pedro Schwartz
Research Monograph 58; ISBN 0 255 36535 7
£12.50

Pricing Our Roads

Vision and Reality
Stephen Glaister & Daniel J. Graham
Research Monograph 59; ISBN 0 255 36562 4
£10.00

The Role of Business in the Modern World

Progress, Pressures, and Prospects for the Market Economy
David Henderson
Hobart Paper 150; ISBN 0 255 36548 9
£12.50

Public Service Broadcasting Without the BBC?

Alan Peacock
Occasional Paper 133; ISBN 0 255 36565 9
£10.00

The ECB and the Euro: the First Five Years

Otmar Issing
Occasional Paper 134; ISBN 0 255 36555 1
£10.00

Towards a Liberal Utopia?

Edited by Philip Booth
Hobart Paperback 32; ISBN 0 255 36563 2
£15.00

The Way Out of the Pensions Quagmire

Philip Booth & Deborah Cooper
Research Monograph 60; ISBN 0 255 36517 9
£12.50

Black Wednesday

A Re-examination of Britain's Experience in the Exchange Rate Mechanism
Alan Budd
Occasional Paper 135; ISBN 0 255 36566 7
£7.50

The Benefits of Tax Competition

Richard Teather
Hobart Paper 153; ISBN 0 255 36569 1
£12.50

Wheels of Fortune

Self-funding Infrastructure and the Free Market Case for a Land Tax
Fred Harrison
Hobart Paper 154; ISBN 0 255 36589 6
£12.50

To order copies of currently available IEA papers, or to enquire about availability, please contact:

Gazelle
IEA orders
FREEPOST RLYS-EAHU-YSCZ
White Cross Mills
Hightown
Lancaster LA1 4XS

Tel: 01524 68765
Fax: 01524 63232
Email: sales@gazellebooks.co.uk

The IEA also offers a subscription service to its publications. For a single annual payment, currently £40.00 in the UK, you will receive every monograph the IEA publishes during the course of a year and discounts on our extensive back catalogue. For more information, please contact:

Adam Myers
Subscriptions
The Institute of Economic Affairs
2 Lord North Street
London SW1P 3LB

Tel: 020 7799 8920
Fax: 020 7799 2137
Website: www.iea.org.uk